Pupils' Perceptions of Europe

Identity and Education

Anne Convery, Michael Evans, Simon Green, Ernesto Macaro and Janet Mellor

CASSELL

Cassell
Wellington House
125 Strand
London WC2R 0BB

PO Box 605
Herndon
VA 20172

First published 1997

British Library Cataloguing-in-Publication Data
A catalogue record for this book is available from the British Library.

ISBN 0-304-33637-8 (hardback)
       0-304-33641-6 (paperback)

Typeset by Action Typesetting Ltd, Gloucester
Printed and bound in Great Britain by Redwood Books, Trowbridge, Wiltshire

Contents

About the Authors

Anne Convery is Lecturer in Education at the School of Education, University of Nottingham

Michael Evans is Lecturer in Education at the School of Education, University of Cambridge

Simon Green is Lecturer in Education and German at Trinity and All Saints University College, Leeds

Ernesto Macaro is Lecturer in Education at the Department of Arts and Humanities in Education, University of Reading

Janet Mellor is Head of the Faculty of Modern Foreign Languages at T. P. Riley Community School, Walsall, formerly Lecturer in Education at the Division of Education, University of Sheffield

Foreword

The outward and visible signs of the bright new world of the European Union are trolleys of duty-free goods pushed through the blue zone of customs halls, and railings in the British press about the iniquities of everyone else in Europe.

These are perhaps a far cry from the belief held by the Secretary of State, expressed in the 1993 schools pack *Education Europe,* that it is 'important for young people to feel that they have a European as well as a local, regional and national identity'. He was right, but neither asserting this truism nor producing a million schools packs make it a reality.

'Feeling European' is more than knowing about the history and the institutions or than understanding a foreign language. It is likely that few of Europe's 350 million citizens will ever respond to the concept in the same way that they respond to being German or Greek. But undoubtedly more positive attitudes must be generated, and this process begins in the schools.

During their research the authors of *Pupils' Perceptions of Europe* have discovered in pupils and teachers a thirst for knowledge and understanding about European politics, institutions and issues. This is a common European phenomenon, recognized by anyone who has had the privilege of observing school links and exchanges over the years, but it is never given much prominence in the various tomes on the European dimension.

The European programmes, Socrates, Leonardo and Youth for Europe, emanating from the Treaty of Maastricht, recognize the centrality of international understanding and the need to overcome national prejudices while at the same time fostering cultural diversity.

The United Kingdom, a mini-Europe of ethnic diversity, is uniquely placed to give a lead in how to carry two or more identities. The opportunity will be missed if xenophobia wins the day. If it does not, the credit will largely be due to schools and colleges, as the authors acknowledge.

There is very little mention of anything European in the English National Curriculum but the authors make a plea for an entitlement to a European dimension, to help people to understand the interrelationship between Europe as a place, a political union, and a home for diverse nations.

This will best be done if youngsters see that the European dimension is not just an interesting idea, though it is that too, but has something in it for them. Some will recognize that lasting peace depends on it. But most will be more impressed by the concrete measures that will give hope to their adult lives.

Already more measures are proposed by the European Commission to try to break up the rigidity of education and training systems and constraining career patterns in the face of the great changes taking place in technology, business and social relations.

A European educational and cultural software industry is proposed. Both actual and virtual mobility will increase. Trans-European projects and courses at many levels and for different purposes will multiply and common approaches to international problems will eventually become the norm. A direct attack on the problems of disaffected young people is proposed.

My spirits are always lifted when talking to colleagues at international meetings. There is a determination to succeed. The hundreds of schools now joining the Comenius school link programme testify to enthusiasm. Schools have started down the road indicated in the EC Ministers' Resolution of October 1992. It begins: 'Education should increase awareness of the growing unity between European peoples and countries and of the establishment of their relations on a new basis.' It ends: 'Young people should be inspired to take an active part in sharing Europe's future.'

There will be resistance on the way, but if 'Europe' does not work together, it will sink together, and, as a born optimist, I do not see the young people of today letting that happen tomorrow. They will need guidance from their teachers, who in turn, will find stimulus in the thinking and research base of *Pupils' Perceptions of Europe*.

Chris Lowe
President, The European Secondary Heads Association
Headmaster, Prince William School, Oundle

Acknowledgements

The authors would like to thank the universities of Cambridge, Nottingham, Sheffield, Reading and Trinity and All Saints University College, as well as the Eastern Region Teacher Education Consortium for providing financial support for the research project at the heart of this book. We are indebted to the teachers in the six countries who welcomed us to their schools, administered the pupil questionnaires, participated in interviews and provided us with insight into the current state of the European dimension in their schools. In particular, our thanks go to: Christine Boré, Antonieta Borrás Marcos, Sue and Jean-Jacques Cichon, Ursula Engeser-Wiebking, J. Geerlings, Franco Greco, Roger Howes, Nick Jones, Cees van der Kooij, Lena Luongo, Barry Mills, Anne O'Reilly, Janet Saddler, Tj. van der Schaaf, Hertha and Heinrich Schilp, Lothar Severin, and Enrique Valdeón. The support of Anunciación Quintero Gallego of the University of Salamanca and Antonia Ruiz Esturla in helping to contact Spanish schools was inestimable. We are also very grateful to Isabel Hernández at the Consejería de Educación in the Spanish embassy for access to documentation and to Jane Restorick at the University of Nottingham for efficiently completing the mammoth task of entering the data onto SPSS.

Finally, none of this would have been possible without the constructive participation of the pupils themselves. The vast majority responded to our intrusion into the routine of their school day with curiosity, bemusement, interest and honesty. If we managed to help them glimpse, however briefly, a fraction of what their future within Europe might entail then our work will need little further justification. It is to them and their peers that this book is dedicated.

Glossary

Area of experience	Broad topic area providing contexts for learning in modern foreign languages in the National Curriculum
ARION	European study visits and exchanges
Central Bureau	Central Bureau for Educational Visits and Exchanges
Childline	Telephone helpline for troubled children in need of counselling
CILT	Centre for Information on Language Teaching and Research
Comenius	Schools Action Programme (1–3) under SOCRATES
CRMLE	Collaborative Research in Modern Languages Education
DES	Department of Education and Science
DFE	Department for Education
DFEE	Department for Education and Employment
EC	European Community
EEC	European Economic Community
ERASMUS	European Action Scheme for the Mobility of University Students
EU	European Union
Euro	European Currency Unit proposed after 1999
FE College	Further Education College (16–19 vocational education in UK)
GDP	Gross Domestic Product
HEI	Higher Education Institution (University of College of Higher Education)
Iron Curtain	Name given to the dividing line between the Communist world and Western Europe by Churchill in 1946
Key Stage 3	Pupils aged 11 to 14 in compulsory schooling in England and Wales
Key Stage 4	Pupils aged 14 to 16 in compulsory schooling in England and Wales
KMK	*Kultusministerkonferenz*: German Education Ministers' Conference
LEA	Local Education Authority
LEONARDO	European programme for vocational training

LINGUA	European initiative on languages training
LOGSE	*Ley Orgánica de Ordenación General del Sistema Educativo*: Spanish educational reform act
MEP	Member of the European Parliament
MFL	Modern Foreign Languages
NC	National Curriculum
NCC	National Curriculum Council
NI	National Insurance
NICC	Northern Ireland Curriculum Council
OECD	Organization for Economic Cooperation and Development
OFSTED	Office for Standards in Education
PGCE	Postgraduate Certificate of Education
PHSE	Personal, Health and Social Education
POS	Programme of Study: what pupils should be taught in each subject in the National Curriculum
PSE	Personal and Social Education
Red Nose Day	aka 'Comic Relief': day set aside for collections for charity in UK
SCAA	School Curriculum and Assessment Authority
SOCRATES	EU Action programme for education
Statutory Orders	Legal requirements under the terms of the National Curriculum
TES/CILT	*Times Educational Supplement* / Centre for Information on Language Teaching and Research
UKCEE	UK Centre for European Education
Y7	Year 7: children aged 11 in compulsory schooling in England and Wales
Y8	Year 8: children aged 12 in compulsory schooling in England and Wales
Y9	Year 9: children aged 13 in compulsory schooling in England and Wales
Y10	Year 10: children aged 14 in compulsory schooling in England and Wales
Y11	Year 11: children aged 15 in compulsory schooling in England and Wales

Introduction

I'm against any type of barrier or any type of exclusion whether it is ideological, political or psychological as long as we conserve the concept that each country will keep its own identity. I hope that it will be school teachers who will be able to help children accept European citizenship. (Italian headteacher)

By the year 2000 many of the children of the baby boom generation will be twenty-one. At the moment they are displaying all the normal characteristics of adolescence: mood swings, optimism suddenly changing into profound pessimism, spontaneity coupled with a desire for stability and security, a yearning to be free from parental control and yet an awareness of the limitations of youth. They have come of age in an era of immense change and rapid development on all fronts. It has been estimated that scientific and technological knowledge alone is doubling every seven years.

The European Union itself is also young and prey to a permanent identity crisis. Post-war Western Europe was born in the early 1950s from a not too auspicious parenthood. After rapid economic growth and expansion it stumbled and staggered through each succeeding decade like a child learning to walk, to speak, and to relate to its family and environment. Landmarks in this development can now be recognized with hindsight: 1957 (the Treaty of Rome); 1973 (membership grows from six to nine states); 1985 (the Single European Act); 1992 (the Maastricht Treaty); 1995 (membership extends to fifteen states). Each landmark agreement was forged out of an entangled mass of mixed sentiments: on the one hand, optimism and idealistic vision; on the other, argument, petulance and dashed hopes. All the emotional swings associated with a young person seeking identity, belonging and a real stake in the world can be linked to this group of states seeking some kind of common ground and some kind of accommodation.

Just how many young people are there in Europe waiting impatiently for adulthood and their stake in society? According to official OECD figures, in 1993 there were 117 million under-25s in the Union's member states. During the 1991/92 academic year there were 67 million pupils and students in the EU – almost one-fifth of the total population. Almost 60 per cent of the under-25s were enrolled in an educational establishment. If we add on those in pre-school education, then nearly 70 per cent of that population group were in some form of education. Nearly 35 million pupils were enrolled in secondary education establishments in the EU in 1991/92, that is to say 52 per cent of all youngsters in education. Across the EU at that time there were also four million teachers engaged in educating all these youngsters and preparing them for the challenges of the next millennium. All these children would grow up 'more or less European' irrespective of the education they received, in the same way as the generations which preceded them have done. However, the creation of the European Union as a political entity has meant that the European awareness of this, and most probably future, generations of young Europeans will be fostered more actively in their schools. The vehicle for instituting this change is, of course, the ill-defined 'European dimension in education'.

Arguably the most significant inter-governmental agreement on the European dimension in education was the Resolution adopted by the Council of Ministers on 24 May 1988. The objectives stipulated in this document (quoted in Chapter 1) are ambitious and extend beyond the acquisition of factual information about Europe and the European Community. Clearly, awareness of Europe and knowledge about its affairs do not necessarily entail support for it. The focus of the ministers' agreement is firmly set on the issue of European identity and citizenship, and calls for the preparation of pupils' future participation in Europe. The objectives explicitly foreground the aim of strengthening in young people 'a sense of European identity' and preparing them to 'take part in the economic and social development of the Community'. However, the means for achieving these objectives remained undefined and responsibility for this was delegated to individual member states. It is interesting to note that in some European countries (notably England and Wales, and Spain) this European initiative coincided with a major national programme of educational reform.

The practical issue of translating the objectives of the Resolution into action through training, funding and curriculum management raised several questions for which there was little central guidance. Most important of all, one must ask, what effect would all of this have upon the recipients of the European dimension in education: namely, the pupils themselves? These questions formed the key part of our research study undertaken five years after the Resolution was first announced to see what impact, if any, it was having upon the pupils of Europe at which it was aimed.

The pupils involved in the research study, which forms the central feature of this book, will have found by the end of the century that they are amongst those who have to keep pace with an unprecedented rate of knowledge advancement and a revolution in communication. Do these youngsters in the European Union see Europe today in the same way as their elders and are their environmental, social and emerging political concerns being taken seriously? What do young people themselves think and feel about the Europe that they are inhabiting at a time of educational and political change? Is there a difference in attitude according to nationality and if so is it due to different political, cultural or educational contexts?

During the last decade policy-makers, educationalists, lecturers and teachers have all provided a wealth of teaching material about the European dimension and governments have put forward several policy initiatives. As a research group made up of lecturers in modern languages education, we wanted to find out the effects of all this activity upon the recipients of such attention and whether there were sources of information (such as the media) which were more or less influential.

The authors of this book, members of a research group called Collaborative Research in Modern Languages Education (CRMLE), met in the summer of 1993 to plan for a cross-national study which attempted to gauge the extent of 14 to 16-year-olds' perceptions of Europe in terms of their knowledge about and their attitudes towards Europe, and to discover the influences on this knowledge and these attitudes. As lecturers in modern languages education we were able to draw on close links with secondary schools in this country as well as corresponding educational contacts on mainland Europe. One of the main early decisions of the project was to carry out the study in a broad range of schools none of which had a reputation or status as a 'European school'. The aim was to find out how pupils were thinking or likely to think about the subject without special input from their institution. In a sense we wanted to find out just how 'European' European children of this age range feel, what this means and why they feel as they do.

The focus from the outset was upon empirical data which would highlight young people's perceptions and these would be compared with official pronouncements upon the place of the European dimension in education in selected European countries.

. We decided early on, as a result of our own interests, language ability, expertise and contacts, to concentrate upon six European countries for our research: England, France, Germany, Spain, Italy and the Netherlands. The bi-annual European Commission publication entitled *Eurobarometer* includes a regular survey of public opinion in European countries on a variety of issues and takes as its sample size 1000 people per country. The focus in those surveys so far had been on tracking adult views on Europe and related issues over Europe since 1973. Little research had been carried out into young people's attitudes to European identity and cooperation.

The pupil questionnaire at the heart of our research project, initially written in English and later translated into the relevant languages, was administered in the six countries in the spring and summer of 1994. It sought to elicit pupils' hitherto largely unexplored views on Europe, on the degree and nature of their European identity, and on the role of the European dimension in their education. We obtained responses from 1337 pupils in total.

In order to understand the reasoning behind the pupils' written answers and to give them an opportunity to talk more freely about their opinions, semi-structured interviews were recorded in England, France, Germany and Italy in the schools where the questionnaires had been administered. However, there was not in all cases a direct link between respondent and interviewee. This did not present a problem, as a remarkable homogeneity revealed itself in interview data per country. A total of 60 interviews were carried out with pupils and some 31 interviews with teachers, deputy heads and head-teachers.

A questionnaire was also subsequently sent to governing bodies (including headteachers, community governors, teacher governors, parent governors and foundation governors) of a representative sample of schools in England in order to elicit their views on the role of the European dimension in education. Forty-five responses were obtained from 37 schools and these are discussed in Chapter 4.

Appended to the pupil questionnaire was a twenty-statement true/false general knowledge quiz which covered a range of European topics including historical, political, geographical, economic and legal matters. The quiz provides, ultimately, a general background to the discussion of the relationship between knowledge and attitudes. It helped to set the attitudes towards Europe (which the pupils expressed in the main part of the questionnaire) against some evidence of their factual knowledge about Europe and the European Union. Given the relative novelty of the name 'European Union' at the time when the questionnaire was administered it was felt that pupils would be more familiar with the term 'EC' than 'EU' and this was used throughout the questionnaire and quiz.

The main thread which runs through this book is the belief that education can and should play an important role in the development of the European dimension of the lives of the citizens of the EU states. Peace in Western Europe since the second world war is not something to be taken lightly and an understanding of the reasons for this stability is something which needs to be grasped by politicians and citizens alike. This understanding also needs to be passed on to succeeding generations so that this peace can be sustained. Allied to this appreciation of the positive aspects of European collaboration is the necessity to confront racial and cultural stereotypes and open them up to critical debate. Chapter 1, 'Understanding the Rhetoric: Policies, Theories and Resolutions', examines the different official conceptions of the European dimension as expressed in the diverse documentation, legislation and official pronouncements which originate from a variety of sources. It focuses upon definitions of the European dimension and highlights the common strands to be found in all these documents: emphasis upon international links, democracy, issues of identity and citizenship. It thus places the CRMLE study in the wider context of other research projects as well as the greater educational and political scene. Providing a critical analysis of the claims of political and educational decision-makers, it serves to make the reality of pupil perceptions more sharply focused and relevant.

The heart of the research study is to be found in Chapter 2, 'Adolescent Perceptions: an Analysis of the CRMLE Research Project'. This provides an in-depth analysis of their attitudes towards Europe, their priorities and aspirations, their perceptions of concepts such as identity and belonging. As the analysis attempts to reveal, educational research in this field has much to learn from parallel empirical studies carried out by social psychologists. Our findings are compared with existing studies of adults' attitudes to Europe. However, the contribution which educational research can make is precisely that of relating pupils' responses to the context of schooling and the nature of different educational sources of influence. We examine the three components of the European dimension (namely, knowledge about Europe, through Europe and for Europe) in the light of the research findings.

Chapter 3, 'Implementing the European Dimension in Secondary Schools: Contexts and Issues', deals with the view from the other side of the classroom. How have teachers and schools generally incorporated the European dimension in the school curriculum? In particular, the chapter looks at the extent to which the different countries have attempted to introduce the European dimension on a subject or cross-curricular basis. The documents of the different national curricula are examined and compared with the comments made by individual teachers about the realities of implementing the stated objectives.

The political implications of the educational debate concerning Europe are broached in Chapter 4, 'The Educational Politics of European Citizenship'. In this chapter the relationship between the European dimension in education and the idea of European citizenship is analysed within the broader context of political education in secondary schools. The National Curriculum in England is critically examined from the point of view of political ideology and the views of governing bodies taken into account. Finally, a proposal is put forward that the European dimension be tackled more from an understanding of process rather than mere subject matter.

Chapter 5, 'Student Teacher Perspectives', is devoted to discussion of the place of the European dimension in the current initial training of secondary school teachers in England and Wales. How far are the teachers of the future prepared to promote the European dimension? What scope is there within the constraints of current PGCE courses to include training on this topic, and in what way does this influence individuals' existing dispositions towards or against Europe? One particular institution is examined as a case study for student teacher perceptions and suggestions are made in the latter part of the chapter to link notions of lifelong learning and continuing professional development to on-going training for all teachers.

Clearly the European dimension in education, like all other subjects in school, is to a large extent dependent upon the overall pedagogical approaches of individual schools and teachers. Where pupils are regarded as passive recipients of information or 'vessels to be filled', then it is likely that any coverage of Europe will be predominantly cognitive, with the emphasis on transmission of factual data about Europe. If, on the other hand, pupils are regarded as 'fires to be lit' then one might expect European awareness to take the form of collaborative projects with partner schools and other means of establishing first-hand contact with Europe. But what are the prerequisites for engaging pupils in an on-going debate about their role as full citizens of Europe and what evidence is there of this happening at the present time? The pupils we surveyed often expressed a desire to know and understand more about the European house that they inhabited. They may have travelled and met some foreigners; they may have seen the news and heard about Eurosquabbles from Spanish fishermen to French farmers, from Brussels bureaucracy to Italian elections. They may also have picked up more sombre news about Bosnia, Chechenia, Northern Ireland, and attacks on asylum seekers in Germany and wondered about this house crumbling at the edges. They had certainly had a rich diet of information; but how much of it had they digested? How much of it did they relate to their own views and aspirations? They had clearly seen and heard much, but was there a consensus of views on Europe and related issues and did it differ from that of adults? How far below the surface of everyday adolescent preoccupations was this consciousness of identity and European citizenship?

It is unlikely that the European dimension in education, as an idea and as a pedagogical issue, is simply going to fade away. It has an internal logic and momentum and finds a sympathetic audience in our research sample. The pupils we surveyed requested much greater transparency, debate and information from their schools and their teachers and we must respond positively to such a request. Chancellor Helmut Kohl stated openly in February 1996 that European integration and closer union were prerequisites for the prevention of war in Europe. The terrorist bomb in London on 9 February 1996 also showed just how fragile some political processes are in the search for peace. Can we any longer afford to neglect the political education of our younger citizens of Europe?

Chapter 1

Understanding the Rhetoric: Policies, Theories and Resolutions

Looking back over his life's work, Jean Monnet, whose vision of a united Europe led to the original economic and trade cooperation taking place between a number of countries in Europe, remarked, 'If I had to start it all again, I would start with education.' This reflection emphasizes the role that education can play in helping to bring people together, for by reviewing his life's work, Monnet was able to identify a means of moving forward. Although education has only latterly come into the European equation, it is steadily assuming a more important position, appearing in all the most recent legislation and documentation, the Maastricht Treaty (1993) being a case in point. The aim of this chapter is to examine critically the plethora of literature which exists on the subject of Europe and the European dimension in education. The intention here is not to trace the historical development of the term 'European dimension', which has already ably been done (Neave, 1984; Mulcahy, 1991), but rather to trace the role which education is playing in the development of the European dimension, thus providing a background to the empirical research project described in Chapter 2 and the discussion in the ensuing chapters. Just as Monnet was led to a realization of the way forward to his goal of a united Europe, it is hoped that a review of the themes, ideas and opinions of writers about Europe and the European dimension will identify some pointers for future developments in education.

A vast amount of literature in the form of both official publications and critical commentaries has been published, mostly in recent years, on the subject of the European dimension in education. Many writers have attempted to define it as a concept and to illustrate their definitions with examples of good practice. The literature can be seen as representing different perspectives and vested interests. On the one hand, European institutions such as the Council of Ministers of Education and the Council of Europe have produced official documents and statements of aims and objectives, requiring responses from individual member states' governments. On the other hand, teachers, lecturers and other professionals working in the field have responded with a myriad of case studies of successful practice and examples of teaching materials, some of which will be examined in Chapter 3. In addition, comparative studies exist which examine different systems and practices across the member states. Reports of European conference proceedings have been published and finally, and perhaps most importantly, a number of texts deal with the philosophical and theoretical debate which continues to rage around the subject of the European dimension.

Very little appears to have been written from the perspective of the younger generation. While the number of schools participating in officially sponsored European projects with 'partner schools' in other countries continues to multiply and attract attention, they remain a minority. There has been scant discussion of the degree and nature of European awareness in the majority of schools. By analysing the detailed views of young people in different European countries, the CRMLE research project hopes to identify areas in need of development and to make recommendations for future policy and practice.

An examination of the various definitions of Europe and the European dimension is essential in order to understand what it is schools are being asked to promote. In order to understand better the term 'European dimension', it is first necessary to examine the idea of Europe itself.

EUROPE

Guy Neave (1984, p. 3) refers to the controversiality of Europe and states that 'there are almost as many interpretations of what "Europe" was, is and ought to be as there are interests arguing about such matters'. In *Teaching about Europe* (1991, p. 22) Margaret Shennan discusses the problems of trying to answer the question 'What is Europe?' She summarizes the controversy which has been going on throughout the centuries between geographers, historians and philosophers and points out that 'the subject can be interpreted at more than one intellectual level'. If we consider the spatial organization of landmass as 'the continent of Europe', the question arises as to where the eastern boundary lies. Prior to 1989, the presence of the Iron Curtain meant that most of our knowledge was focused on Western Europe and the countries of the EU, but the emergence of the eastern bloc countries has led to a reappraisal of what constitutes Europe. Shennan, referring to 'the limitations of a rigid geographical definition', suggests the notion of a dynamic and diverse Europe, whose people share 'common beliefs, values and ways of life' (pp. 25–6).

Writers on the subject of Europe are often at great pains to clarify the distinction between the wider notion of the continent of Europe and the narrower definition of the European Union. Witold Tulasiewicz (King and Reiss, 1993) points out that 'confining the European Dimension to the European Community (EC) may help to present a more compact whole, but it is also open to the accusation that it ignores the rest of the world' (p. 241). This view is expressed even more forcefully by Sultana (1995). The danger of having a Eurocentric focus, or 'fortress Europe' approach is mentioned by several writers as being counter-productive to the aims and objectives of the European dimension. For example, an EMIE/NFER report of 1991 puts it this way: 'European Awareness should not mean for our young people a replacement of "Little Englanderism" by "little Europeanism". It should be the first step towards an understanding of what it means to be a citizen of the world, to understand the issues that ultimately affect us all' (p. 10). Heater (1992), on the other hand, makes a distinction between 'awareness' about Europe as a whole and 'European citizenship' which he sees as firmly tied to the EU where a legal-political status can only be exercised through the context of a polity. However, Tulasiewicz goes a stage further when he states that it should also include 'all those recent Europeans who live in Europe but whose roots are in Morocco, Bangladesh or Turkey' (p. 241).

The idea of perception as opposed to reality is introduced in the opening paragraph of the Metropolitan Borough of Knowsley's European Policy for Schools (1994):

> A European entity is not easily defined by commonly accepted criteria. Whatever lines are drawn on the political map, the fact remains that it is the perception as much as the reality which defines a 'European'. It is an area of political philosophy which is driven by its own intentions and more importantly by the willingness of people to see the horizon as something to be crossed rather than as a boundary to preserve their own insularity. In itself it can appear both liberal and reactionary, eurocentric and global, centralist and divergent.

By referring to horizons and boundaries, and by citing some key problem areas, the writer appears to have captured the true essence of Europe in the last decade of the twentieth century.

THE EUROPEAN DIMENSION

If there is difficulty in defining the term 'Europe', there is no less difficulty in explaining what is meant by the European dimension. Two approaches to the European dimension can be distinguished. First, a 'prescriptive' approach of the kind found in policy statements and official documents issued by European, national and local bodies and, second, a more 'explorative' approach favoured by writers and researchers in the fields of education and social science.

Mulcahy (1991), in his aptly named article 'In Search of the European dimension in education', traces the idea and understanding of the term from its conception in the 1977 Community policy statement 'Towards a European education policy', up until the landmark Resolution of the Council of Ministers of Education, of 24 May 1988, and the individual member states' policy statements which followed. Mulcahy refers to the progress made by the Community in having 'its own ideal of the kind of education needed to sustain its aspirations as a community' (p. 213), which is no longer the economic community of its inception in 1957, but 'more integrated as a social and cultural community also'. As attention began to focus on a more integrated community, activities promoting pupil mobility and exchange, language teaching, international schools, teacher mobility and teacher training all gained recognition. According to Mulcahy, 'teaching about Europe and about the Community was being conceived in cross-disciplinary and experiential terms', characterized by a 'boldness and freshness of approach' (p. 216).

In the 1990s, the level of debate of the European dimension has increased, and as new directives and policy statements are being issued, so the understanding of the term is changing and developing. Maitland Stobart (in Shennan, 1991) sees the European dimension as a dynamic and evolving concept, involving education in Europe, education about Europe and education for Europe. This idea is mirrored in a Council of Europe working paper prepared by the Education Committee of the Council for Cultural Cooperation (Vienna, 1991) which, when referring to the European dimension of education, states that it has 'evolved since the early post-war years from a limited, civics-style approach to one that involves preparing all young people for international contact and mobility on a major scale for the purposes of work, study and leisure in the wider community of Europe and the rest of the world. It can be seen as a dynamic, evolving, multifaceted concept involving political, economic, social and cultural aspects'.

Feneyrou (1993, pp. 31–9) outlines a temporal view when considering the European dimension, or 'significant aspects of Europe', namely: 'the past – historic ties between member countries, their community of origin, the present – the current ties, the economic, political and cultural community (our present) and the future of Europe, the common interests of the member countries'. Feneyrou also discusses the concepts of nationality and identity, both national and European, and asks the reader to consider if there is indeed a European cultural identity. A striking, though perhaps understandable, feature of much of the literature in this field is the writers' propensity to ask questions. As many questions are posed as answers given, which again reflects the evolving nature of the concept of the European dimension, referred to earlier.

The idea that the European dimension is about more than facts was put forward by Neave (1984), who argues that teaching is not enough, unless it includes 'the notion of educating for "European citizenship" as an integral part of their programme' (p. 120). The notion of education for citizenship is one which has only relatively recently received closer scrutiny, and it will be considered further, later in this chapter.

Margaret McGhie (1993) refers to the 'difficult question' of defining the European dimension. She draws an interesting distinction between European perspective and European dimension. The former is seen as a process of sensitization to different cultures, attitudes, behaviours and beliefs in order to develop a European identity, whereas the latter is defined as 'an attitude of mind based on a set of principles, guide-lines or values' to 'help us all towards an understanding of unity in diversity and of our responsibilities as citizens of Europe' (p. 33). The European dimension, as defined by McGhie, clearly makes a strong link with the notion of citizenship, and the obligations that it entails.

For Brock and Tulasiewicz (1994) the European dimension consists of European knowledge – for pupils to be better informed about the continent of Europe – European skills (linguistic, communication, social, negotiation, travel), and European attitudes, enabling pupils to confirm a commitment to Europe. This idea reflects Stobart's 'in, about and for Europe' definition, with European knowledge being 'about Europe', European skills being necessary 'in Europe' and European attitudes being necessary 'for Europe'. A similar idea is postulated by Tulasiewicz (1993) when defining the scope of the European dimension, which includes 'disparate elements, such as knowledge, skills, attitudes and commitments taught at different times and under different headings' (p. 244).

Shennan (1991, p. 21) regards the European dimension in the curriculum as a process leading to an improvement in 'the quality and breadth of pupil knowledge by making Europe a new focal point of normal school experience'. With regard to the school curriculum, Knowsley's European Policy for Schools (1994), the principles of which are reproduced here, encapsulates in accessible language many of the themes, ideas and concepts already referred to in this chapter:

- The European dimension should be an integral part of the curriculum.
- The European Dimension refers to all those countries within recognised political and geographical boundaries called Europe. As such the dimension should reflect the variety

of political, social, economic, cultural, racial and religious characteristics in Europe.
- It is essential to provide opportunities for young people in Knowsley to develop the knowledge, understanding, skills and attitudes to enable them to participate in the community of Europe.
- The European Dimension should be concerned with deepening young people's knowledge and understanding of other countries and their people; and in doing so challenge ill-informed perceptions and stereotyping. This should also provide opportunities for young people to reflect upon their own society's history, culture and values.
- The European Dimension should be considered in the context of global issues, and provide a means of addressing issues, such as Multiculturalism and Equal Opportunities.

The distinction made by Stobart concerning education 'in, about and for Europe', referred to earlier in this chapter, can be recognized in the Knowsley principles. 'In Europe' is reflected in the statement about young people being enabled to participate in the community of Europe. 'About Europe' links to the second and fourth principles quoted above and the notion of 'for Europe' is found in the fourth and fifth principles. In 1992, a spokesperson at the Department for Education, London, referred to the European dimension as 'a phrase cloaked in mystery'! It would appear that in Knowsley's European policy an attempt has been made to disperse the mystery and to provide a working definition of the European dimension which will form a sound basis for understanding by a wide readership (advisors, teachers, parents, governors), followed by interpretation and implementation in schools.

OFFICIAL GUIDELINES AND LEGISLATION

The impetus for a greater understanding of what is meant by the term 'European dimension' came from a Resolution adopted by the Council of Ministers of Education on 24 May 1988. A series of measures to be carried out at both member states level and community level was launched with a view to strengthening the European dimension in education.

The text of the Resolution objectives is as follows:

- strengthen in young people a sense of European identity and make clear to them the value of European civilization and of the foundations on which the European peoples intend to base their development today, that is in particular the safeguarding of the principles of democracy, social justice and respect for human rights;
- prepare young people to take a part in the economic and social development of the Community and in making concrete progress towards European union, as stipulated in the Single European Act;
- make them aware of the advantages which the Community represents, but also of the challenges it involves, in opening up an enlarged economic and social area to them;
- improve their knowledge of the Community and its member states in their historical, cultural, economic and social aspects and bring home to them the significance of the cooperation of the member states of the European Community with other countries of Europe and the World.

The Resolution can be seen as illustrative of the 'prescriptive' approach referred to earlier, and certainly contains elements of the 'in, about and for Europe' definition proposed by Stobart. Following the objectives, the measures to be carried out at member states level were the incorporation of the European dimension into educational systems, school programmes and teaching, teaching materials, teacher training, contacts between pupils and teachers from different countries and complementary measures (for example, colloquia, seminars, European clubs, European Schools Days, sporting events). As a follow-up to the Resolution, member states were required to publish their own policy statements on the European dimension in education, together with a report of activity undertaken to implement it. This, in turn, was reported on in a Commission document, SEC (91) 1753, published in September 1991, which summarizes the action taken by the member states and by the European Community, and contains a follow-up and assessment of the action taken (European Commission, 1991). Broadly speaking, this report reveals similar findings across the member states (Tulasiewicz, 1993) but different aspects are stressed by different states. Three ideas which are pursued by all member states are the Community ideal, a humanist ideal and an international perspective. Each theme will now be examined in more detail, drawing examples from the government responses of the member states involved in the CRMLE study.

The Community ideal entails a range of assimilative notions such as belonging, citizenship, identity and integration. In the Dutch government's response, for example, published in April 1989, and 'primarily intended for the European Community and its member states', it is claimed that 'the expected goals of the Resolution are to actively prepare the citizen for life in Europe after 1992'. The German government's response, from the *Kultusministerkonferenz* (KMK), was issued in December 1990 and is entitled *Europa im Unterricht* ('Europe in the Classroom'). In it is represented the idea of the harmonization of common social and economic policies of member states, so that 'Europe's citizens are increasingly coming to experience and understand Europe as a common house in which vital developments concerning their lives are taking place ... a house which they have to build and maintain together.' Furthermore, the role of education is to 'arouse young people's awareness of a European identity. This also involves preparing young people to fulfil their tasks as citizens in the European Community.' The UK government's response, published in February 1991, does not explicitly refer to the notion of citizenship, but instead talks of 'preparing young people to take part in the economic and social development of Europe' and of 'promoting a sense of European identity'. The Spanish government's response, also issued in 1991, includes in its policy aims the need to 'explore the European dimension of our cultural roots'. Indeed the preamble to the new reform of the Spanish educational system (LOGSE, 1990) sets the whole enterprise within the framework of a 'common European horizon'.

The humanist ideal of the member states' responses centres on the values and attitudes of peace, human rights, freedom, democracy and understanding. The French government's Education Act of July 1989 states that the European dimension 'must help to develop a knowledge of other cultures', while the UK statement refers to 'helping pupils and students to acquire a view of Europe as a multi-cultural, multi-lingual community which includes the UK'. The German response details a Europe 'in which all countries and peoples will be able to achieve self-determination in freedom'. Furthermore, 'a comprehensive dialogue is taking place on questions of human rights ... and disarmament'. The Spanish response lists the 'internal market, social justice, human rights, and political and democratic structures' as thematic areas for coverage through the European dimension.

The third common theme which occurs in all the member states' responses is that of an international perspective, based on multi-culturalism, solidarity and intercultural education. The Dutch policy states that 'we would like to see a Europe which is broader than its trade barriers' and furthermore, 'we would internationalise by exchanging teacher trainers and forging international links'. The UK policy reflects an outward-looking perspective by 'promoting an understanding of the EC's interdependence with the rest of Europe, and with the rest of the world'. The German statement makes the strongest appeal in this respect, challenging Europeans to 'appreciate other people's perspectives, to be tolerant, to express solidarity and to practise coexistence with people who speak different languages and have other customs. Europeans must recognise the responsibility for freedom, peace, justice and social balance placed in their hands – above all with regard to the developing countries'. The Spanish government's policy refers to the necessity of 'showing solidarity with countries of Eastern Europe or countries having specific characteristics e.g. Atlantic and Mediterranean', whilst the Italian policy calls for a Europe 'working to consolidate a culture of communication and development to make the Europe of the cultures transcend that built on economy and trade'.

Following on from the three themes dealt with in the preceding paragraphs, member states' policies also commented on school curricula and educational systems, teaching materials and the mobility of pupils and teachers. These areas will now be briefly surveyed, again drawing examples from the government responses of the countries included in the CRMLE research. The issue of teacher training will be addressed in Chapter 5.

All the member states were in agreement that the European dimension should not be delivered through a separate course, but that it should be integrated into appropriate curricular areas. The Dutch policy states 'we do not wish to set up Europe as a separate subject', whilst it is the UK government's view that 'appreciation and understanding of the European dimension cannot best be achieved through a discrete European studies course in the curriculum'. The German policy is that 'all fields of learning in the school can make a contribution to developing the European dimension'. The document then goes on to enumerate all the subjects in the curriculum (and it is virtually the whole curriculum) which offer 'opportunities for specialist work or work transcending traditional subject boundaries', namely geography, history, social studies/politics, economics, law, languages, mathematics, natural sciences, technology, religion, philosophy, art, music, sport and classics. This impressive list is not repeated by the other countries, who mostly view the European dimension as being appropriately considered through geography, history and modern languages. Exactly how the European dimension is intended to be delivered in the UK, and what actually happens in practice, will be dealt with more fully in Chapter 3. French policy emphasizes a gradual raising of awareness of European matters, through cultural, literary and socio-economic aspects. Spanish policy makes reference to an explicit coverage of the European dimension and cites the problem of ethics in natural sciences as an example. Italian policy rejects the idea of teaching only facts about Europe and prefers an approach which is 'a dynamic process involving the quest for methodological and teaching strategy and subject matter already shared throughout the European culture'.

With regard to teaching materials, all member states were in agreement as to their importance in incorporating a European dimension in schools. The Dutch policy statement referred to a survey which showed that 'Europe is scarcely given attention in textbooks', but noted that 'freedom of education forces the Dutch government to tread carefully'. However, a regular need for updated information and an overview of available documentation was noted. Similarly, in the UK, 'there is no central control of teaching material. Where the European dimension forms part of the National Curriculum subject or is otherwise included in the school curriculum, the text books and other teaching materials for the subjects concerned would also reflect the European dimension'. In the German policy, reference to teaching materials is made in a series of recommendations for further development: 'Improvement of basic information on Europe, European cooperation and integration and on European inter-relationships in all specialist teaching and educational material intended for both the teacher and the pupil' and 'ensuring that "the European dimension in the classroom" is included in the examination criteria when authorizing teaching and learning material'.

One final action point of the Resolution worthy of discussion in this context is the mobility of pupils and teachers. In the UK, the Central Bureau administers a large network of school contacts and exchanges, and the exchange tradition is well developed: 'Since 1988 the Schools Unit of the Central Bureau has set up 487 new school and college links with partner institutions in other European countries.' The Central Bureau is also responsible for organizing study visits, short courses and teacher exchange schemes, as well as a foreign-language-assistant programme. In the Netherlands 'some schools have made interesting initiatives such as educational projects which are combined with exchanges', whilst in Germany 'the exchange of pupils and teachers is important. This should be practised with as many European countries as possible'. One of the recommendations for further development involves 'improvement of teachers' and pupils' motivation to deal with European questions by gathering their own first hand experience of Europe (increased participation in bilateral exchanges, encounters, project measures and foreign language practice)'. Furthermore, school partnerships are to be encouraged, with Central and Eastern Europe being singled out for a special mention.

While considering the member states' responses to the Resolution of 24 May 1988, it must not be forgotten that the content of such a resolution is not legally enforceable, and that the responses rely on the commitment and good will of the individual governments to carry them out. The responses must, therefore, be judged bearing that fact in mind. The question then arises: 'Are the responses to be judged separately or as a whole?' The report on the member states' responses referred to earlier (European Commission, 1991) draws attention to the 'substantial diversity' of the documents, although it concludes that, 'all made an effort to implement the Resolution'. Whilst no one would wish to sacrifice the diversity contained within the responses, if, as the report indicates, 'certain aspects may have been stressed to the detriment of others', then it may be that lack of a commonly acknowledged and shared vision could be counter-productive. The speed with which the individual responses to the Resolution were published could be interpreted as an indication of the amount of commitment felt by the member states' governments. For example, the Dutch response appeared in April 1989, less than a year after the publication of the Resolution, and the French response appeared in July 1989. The German response appeared in December 1990, although this report was based largely on a previous document of 1978, and the Germans could claim to have been ahead of the field by at least a decade. The Germans were also preoccupied from November 1989 to October 1990 with unification. The December 1990 document contains views from all sixteen *Bundesländer*, including the five newly acquired ones. The UK response appeared in February 1991.

Taking the response of the UK government as a further example, it is interesting to note the similarities and differences between its text (reproduced below) and that of the Resolution (see page 5):

The UK government has been and will continue to be active in promoting the objectives of the EC Resolution on the European dimension in education. The government's policies are aimed at:

- helping pupils and students to acquire a view of Europe as a multi-cultural, multi-lingual community which includes the UK;
- encouraging awareness of the variety of European histories, geographies and cultures;
- preparing young people to take part in the economic and social development of Europe and making them aware of the opportunities and challenges that arise;
- encouraging interest in and improving competence in other European languages;
- imparting knowledge of political, economic and social developments, past, present and future, including knowledge about the origins, workings and role of the EC;
- promoting a sense of European identity, through first hand experience of other countries where appropriate;
- promoting an understanding of the EC's interdependence with the rest of Europe, and with the rest of the world.

If the texts of the two documents are compared, some dilution of the strength of the language has taken place in the UK government's response. The phrase 'strengthen in young people a sense of European identity' becomes 'promoting a sense of European identity'. In addition, the phrase 'make clear to them the value of European civilization' becomes 'encouraging awareness of the variety of European histories, geographies, and cultures'. Again, the positive mention of 'advantages and challenges' becomes a more reserved 'opportunities and challenges' in the UK document. Other subtle differences can be perceived and it must also be stated that there is more concentration on the 'in and about Europe' part of Stobart's definition, than on the 'for Europe' aspect. The Resolution promotes the 'safeguarding of the principles of democracy, social justice and respect for human rights', an aspect of Stobart's 'for Europe' definition, whereas the UK text does not include such a mention. These differences in interpretation most likely reflect the political climate in the UK at the time (and currently), in which the Eurosceptic lobby is a powerful and vociferous one, and one which is more frequently and persuasively voiced in the media. The question of how far this is proving to be an obstacle to the way forward in UK educational spheres will be addressed in Chapter 3.

Since the member states' governments' responses are interim statements only, the following questions must be asked: What has happened since 1991? Has development taken place? Have the interim reports been updated? One important development and the most recent one in terms of the European dimension in education has been the ratification of the Maastricht Treaty in 1993.

THE MAASTRICHT TREATY

This is a major piece of community legislation in which education has appeared for the first time. The text of the articles concerned with education (126, non-vocational education and 127, vocational education) are printed in full in Appendix E1, but the main points are those which were previously dealt with in the Resolution of 24 May 1988: the European dimension, the mobility of students and teachers, cooperation between educational establishments, the exchange of information and experience between member states, the development of youth exchanges and the development of distance education. It is interesting to remark that these points are primarily concerned with 'in and about Europe' and that there is no mention here of the 'for Europe' principles such as democracy and human rights, which were important in the Resolution of 24 May 1988. These issues are referred to in other parts of the treaty, but are not specifically linked to the education chapters. It is also significant that the teaching and dissemination of the languages of the member states is introduced here. It was not mentioned at all in the Resolution, but occurred in the UK response, which referred to 'encouraging interest in and improving competence in other European languages'. It would appear that the education chapters are functional and practical in focus, with little reference to the humanist ideals and principles which characterized the Resolution and succeeding member states' responses. The international perspective of the Commission document SEC (91) 1753, which raised the issues of multiculturalism, solidarity and intercultural education is not found here, either. Thus, the European dimension now has a legislative framework within which to operate, but since the principle of subsidiarity will prevail ('excluding any harmonization of the laws and regulations of the Member States', Article 126), it will be interesting to observe over the coming years exactly how the laws are put into practice.

CITIZENSHIP

Provision was also made in the Maastricht Treaty for the inclusion of articles conferring citizenship of the Union on the individual nationals of all the member states (Articles 8–8d, see Appendix E2). The notion of citizenship can be linked back to the first of the three themes which were identified by the writers of the document discussed on page 6 (European Commission, 1991b). This Community ideal picks up the assimilative themes of integration, belonging and identity which had been raised by several of the member states.

Although European identity has been represented in the UK media as posing a threat to national identity, the new concept is not intended to weaken national identities. It is intended to create new rights and benefits, and to work towards the whole process of integration. These new rights will enable citizens to vote and stand as candidates in local and European elections in EU countries other than their own, permit them to take complaints to a new EU ombudsman, and finally, to receive wider diplomatic protection outside the EU.

The concept of European citizenship is not a new one, however. According to *Maastricht Made Simple* (*The European*, 1992), the concept has been grappled with for the past twenty years in European documentation and at summits, conferences and other meetings. In the same way as the terms 'Europe' and 'European dimension' have been discussed and defined, so too has the term 'European citizenship'. As referred to earlier in this chapter, some writers see the notion of citizenship being firmly situated within the European dimension (Neave, 1984, McGhie, 1993). Dekker analyses the concept of European citizenship, traces the development of the concept over thirty years through EC policy reports and other official pronouncements and examines some of the data available through EC-commissioned surveys and research concerning the opinions and attitudes of young people to various aspects of European citizenship. He concludes, 'the long-term survival of the present European Community and the development of a yet more integrated "European Union" will only be possible if the majority of the citizens possess knowledge about "European" matters, are convinced of the intrinsic importance and value of an integrated Europe, are prepared to identify themselves with such a Europe and are prepared and willing to contribute to its realization' (Dekker, 1993, pp. 41–56). Starkey (1995, p. 21) draws the same conclusions, expressed more simply: 'citizenship implies feeling committed to the community as well as simply knowing about it. Education for European citizenship has to be based on thinking, feeling and doing'. The concept of citizenship is developed more fully in the context of the CRMLE research project in Chapter 4.

PREVIOUS RESEARCH INTO YOUNG PEOPLE'S ATTITUDES TO EUROPE

Although much has been written on the subject of the European dimension in education from a theoretical point of view, relatively little is known about the views of young people in Europe. A number of official surveys and studies have been carried out on behalf of the European Commission and published in the *Eurobarometer* series. Three such studies are called *The Young Europeans* (1982), *Young Europeans in 1987* (1989) and *Young Europeans in 1990* (1991), with each study based on data collected in ten or twelve member states from between 3867 and 7600 young people, aged between 15 and 24. Questions were asked based on the young people's EC knowledge, their opinions on membership of the EC and the Single Market, their attitudes towards European issues and citizenship and their behavioural intentions concerning their European franchise.

Some of the questions asked in the *Eurobarometer* surveys were similar to ones asked in the CRMLE survey, and it is worth examining briefly the answers to these questions, so that they may act as a point of comparison for the CRMLE data, described in Chapter 2. Since the surveys were instigated by the European Commission, the questions related specifically to the EC. In the sections based on their EC knowledge, most young people did not feel themselves sufficiently well-informed. For example, in 1990, 16 per cent of young people felt well-informed about the EC and 72 per cent wanted to know more. In the sections on their opinions on membership of the EC and the Single Market, in 1982 40 per cent of the young people surveyed would have favoured decisions in important areas being taken at a European and not at a national level. The CRMLE survey probes this area in greater depth. With regard to their attitudes to the EC, the young people were not overly positive or enthusiastic. For example, closer European unity as a cause worthy of risk-taking and sacrifices was perceived only by a tiny majority (8 per cent in 1982, 8 per cent in 1987 and 12 per cent in 1990) as being important. The CRMLE survey explores certain issues of closer European unity in greater depth. A further area of investigation of the *Eurobarometer* surveys was concerned with nationality and identity. In 1982, 65 per cent of young Europeans said they were very or quite proud of their nationality. In the same survey 15 per cent of young people often thought of themselves as a European citizen. The same questions were probed in the CRMLE study. The results of the *Eurobarometer* surveys could not be said to be overly positive in terms of the young people's knowledge about, opinions of and attitudes to Europe.

There have been fewer studies into the views of young people which have not been commissioned by the European Commission. One such study, entitled 'Students' attitudes to Europe', was carried out in 1992, by Bordas and Giles Jones (Bordas and Giles Jones, 1993, pp. 89–111), who administered questionnaires to 834 pupils between the ages of 11 and 19 in eight EC countries. The pupils did not represent a random sample, since the schools selected were ones in which participants in a teacher training module were carrying out their teaching practice or were likely to be employed in the future. Similar questions to the ones used in the *Eurobarometer* surveys were asked, namely, concerning knowledge of Europe, interest in Europe, experience of Europe and attitudes and feelings towards Europe. The questions focus on a wider definition of Europe than the EC although Europe is not defined as such, but left open to the students' interpretations.

In terms of their knowledge about Europe, 50.5 per cent of the young people in the Bordas and Giles Jones survey admitted that they did not have much knowledge about Europe. On the other hand, an encouraging 85.5 per cent stated that they would like to know more about Europe. Similar questions are asked in the CRMLE study. Travel was found to be important in the pupils' lives; all those surveyed had travelled to either another country in the EC or in other parts of Europe. Nationality and identity were again areas of interest – 40 per cent of the pupils surveyed thought of themselves as both European and a citizen of their own country. In terms of the curriculum, modern languages, geography and history were the three subjects where pupils felt that they learned the most about the European dimension. All these areas are explored in the CRMLE study.

Another survey, which was carried out and reported in the *Independent* on 11 July 1994 by Public Voice International (PVI), a Bristol-based research organization, asked 2000 pupils in the county of Avon what kind of future they wanted for Britain. The results showed that a majority (31 per cent of the pupils) envisaged a Euro-Britain, where Britain had much closer ties with the rest of Europe even if this meant some loss of independence. This was a useful project, though on a limited scale since only British pupils were targeted, and since the focus was not Europe or the EC, but rather the future choices for Britain. Some of the questions in this survey were of relevance, however. When asked to identify from a list their perception of the three greatest threats to Britain, 9 per cent highlighted Britain getting left out of a United Europe, 13 per cent selected the war in the former Yugoslavia spreading to other countries in Europe, and 20 per cent opted for extreme or racist parties getting stronger in Britain and in the rest of Europe. When asked if pupils thought that Britain should work more closely with the rest of Europe, even if it meant losing some of their national identity, students were evenly divided between those in favour (32 per cent), those not in favour (36 per cent) and those who did not know (32 per cent). All these surveys help to define a background against which the CRMLE research can be set.

FURTHER RESEARCH NEEDS

The paucity of empirical data concerning the attitudes of the younger generation towards Europe, especially in the form of research carried out independently of official European structures, is emphasized by several writers. Ken Fogelman (in Edwards, Munn and Fogelman, 1994) calls for research to be carried out due to urgent concerns with young people who may be 'politically ignorant, cynical, distrustful of politics and politicians, and whose loyalties are tribal'. He outlines the need for research into the 'current state of political and social knowledge, beliefs, attitudes and values' of young people, adding that there are 'some individual countries where research to answer such questions is in hand, but their value would be multiplied if there were some coordination to provide international comparability and comparisons' (p. 14). Dekker (1993) finds that there is 'a strong need for more research with respect to European citizenship, socialization and education' and concludes that 'finding out why socialization for European citizenship in general and education for European citizenship in particular have a limited effect and how to improve the quality of actions in this field would be in the interest of both the EC elites and individual citizens and in the interest of popular democracy as well' (p. 52). From a slightly different angle, Prucha (in Endt and Lenaerts, 1993) finds that 'empirical studies are necessary to compare factual knowledge, attitudes and values shared by students in particular countries' (p. 29). Prucha also suggests that research be carried out to describe an 'attitude profile' of pupil and student populations for the qualities of European awareness. In conclusion, Fogelman (in Edwards, Munn and Fogelman, p. 20) identifies the need for 'national and international surveys of the knowledge, beliefs and activities of young people' together with 'longitudinal studies of how these develop'.

CONCLUSIONS

After all the official documents, legislation and discursive arguments have been read and digested, where does this leave the reader in terms of an understanding of the European dimension? What steps should now be taken? Are the official pronouncements having an effect at grass roots level? The review of the literature on Europe and the European dimension reveals the inherent difficulties in arriving at a commonly held understanding. Perhaps this is not even desirable? What is clear is the distinction between the texts which tell us what we should be doing and those in which the emphasis is more on discovery and interaction. Certainly, the 'in, about and for Europe' definition seems to be a very helpful one, especially when linked to the idea of European knowledge, skills and attitudes.

There is no doubt that the Resolution of 24 May 1988 has had far-reaching effects, both in the member states' responses and in the literature which has appeared since then. However, the question must be reiterated: At which levels are the pronouncements being effective? Are young people in Europe gaining the knowledge, skills and attitudes necessary to help them assume their European citizenship? There is currently a paucity of research to examine in order to answer such questions. Such as there is appears now to be dated or not to be on a large enough scale to be convincing. Several writers have made strong pleas for further research to be carried out, and it would appear that the time is now apposite for this to happen.

The main body of this chapter details the climate, background and context against which the CRMLE research took place. In view of the calls for international comparability studies into the knowledge, skills and attitudes of young people in Europe, the CRMLE study is a timely response and should provide valuable empirical evidence which may answer some of the questions raised here. It is hoped that, from the data and evidence collected, a more informed evaluation of what the European dimension means to young people can be offered. Being informed about what young people think and know about Europe may help the policy makers to judge the effectiveness of their policies and may challenge the perceived wisdom of current approaches to the European dimension in the curriculum.

Chapter 2

Adolescent Perceptions of Europe: An Analysis of the CRMLE Research Study

We are the 'new generation' and as adults we are going to live in this world. It's normal we want to know more about the future. We are badly informed about 'our Europe' which belongs to us all. (A French pupil's reason for wanting to learn and understand more about Europe.)

At first glance, the idea of Europe, in all its guises and conceptions, may seem at a very far remove from the concerns, priorities and passions of the world of adolescents. One might be excused for thinking that an empirical study on the subject would meet with universal indifference and suspicion on the part of youngsters surveyed and that consequently it would be likely to result in predictably barren outcomes. Can there be a more salient example of a current issue represented, debated and decided upon exclusively by adults? 'Europe' as an institution is a construct invented and operated by politicians, bureaucrats, employers, educationalists and other categories of the primarily professional class who largely determine the boundaries of the lives and opportunities of all citizens including, and perhaps especially, of young people who have not yet reached adulthood.

Yet looked at more closely, and as the few projects that have been carried out testify (see, for example, Bordas and Giles Jones, 1993; Patterson and Sahni, 1994), the majority of teenagers respond to the topic with interest, a degree of frustration about not being sufficiently informed, and a desire to know more. The French teenager quoted at the start of this chapter firmly expresses the view, felt by many other young people in Europe, that Europe represents part of their future. A possible explanation of this unexpected level of interest may be that Europe is currently in the process of self-definition and development and therefore that the topic is concerned with change and the future, a perspective which tends to attract the younger generation who are less rooted in the traditions and experiences of the past. In a sense, a cross-national search for identity and maturation mirrors the parallel personal questionings and developmental processes experienced by adolescents. Europe, as an institution, is itself at an adolescent stage.

Secondly, discussion about Europe often entails discussion of specific socio-political issues such as the environment, health, animal welfare and other topics which currently attract young people. 'Single issue politics' currently popular amongst young adults in the UK suggests an attachment to practical, social or humanitarian issues divorced, in many cases, from traditional party political allegiances. The European context can, for the moment at least, provide a framework for pupils' exploration of such issues.

Both these possible explanations suggest that it is the process of discussion and enquiry which acts as the key to engaging young people's interest in the topic. Simply lecturing pupils about Europe or handing them glossy official documents will not cut much ice; on the other hand, talking to them about social priorities, work and travel opportunities, national and cultural allegiances and preferred levels of political decision-making on different issues can successfully engage pupils' interest. The difference is between a participative approach and a didactic one. In this way, too, the European dimension becomes an example of what Bruner called ' "means–ends" knowledge': that is, 'knowledge that brings into a single focus the two kinds of relevance, personal and social' (Bruner, 1974, p. 131). Similar distinctions have been made about conceptions of citizenship in general (for instance, by Henk Dekker (1994, p. 52) who distinguishes between 'communal' and 'contractual' theories of citizenship) and of citizenship education (for instance, by T. H. McLaughlin (1992, p. 237) who compares 'minimalist' and 'maximalist' interpretations of citizenship education). Similarly, in their discussion of citizenship education, Engle and Ochoa (1988) make a parallel distinction between content and process: 'a problem-solving curriculum combines the ideas related to social issues and conditions (content) with an intellectual and values dimension (process) to develop higher level thinking and decision-making skills' (p. 178). We shall look in more detail at the politics and pragmatics of organizing the promotion of European awareness within different subjects (for instance, politics, social studies or civics) in later chapters, but the initial starting-point for pupils in the upper secondary school across Europe would seem to be that thinking about Europe allows them to redefine their identities in new ways and to test their existing loyalties and convictions.

It is just such a 'starting-point' which the present chapter aims to analyse in the light of the findings of the recent research study conducted by the authors of this book.

DIFFERENT PERSPECTIVES IN RESEARCHING ATTITUDES TO EUROPE

There are clearly different ways in which attitudes and perceptions to a topic such as Europe can be elicited. The most direct approach is to ask pupils openly about the extent to which they identify with Europe, setting aside, temporarily, questions about definition. This has the merit of outlining the strength of an individual's attachment to the identity. It represents an affective preference. Alternatively, one can ask pupils to choose from ready-made definitions. In their survey, Bordas and Giles Jones asked pupils to select their definition of Europe from a brief list presented in the question-naire. They found that 41 per cent considered Europe mainly 'a civilization' and 39.5 per cent considered it 'the Common Market'. The authors concluded that 'the percep-tion of Europe as a "community", that is, as a group of people who live together and cooperate with one another, is not very widespread'. This approach does presuppose, though, that terms like 'civilization' and 'community' are understood in the same way by all respondents regardless of class, culture, nationality or intellectual ability. Third, one can adopt a more indirect approach and attempt to look more closely at specific reactions to issues and possible scenarios in order to paint a fuller picture of how a pupil feels about practicalities relating to Europe. The object of enquiry here is not their attitudes towards dominant images and conceptions of Europe but towards the socio-political changes affecting their lives which could ensue.

A fourth approach, adopted by developmental psychologists, is primarily cognitive in nature and analyses children's mental conceptions of other European nationals. A recent English study on this topic, carried out by Martin Barret and Janis Short (1992), examined the nature of the attitudes of 216 5 to 10-year-old English schoolchildren towards French, German, Spanish and Italian people. The study suggests that the process of stereotyping foreign nationals begins very early on (in many cases from the age of 5) and that consequently there is a need to counterbalance the early entrenchment of prejudice or negative attitudes among children through education. Further, their study revealed that the 8 to 10-year-old children in the sample 'tended to agree upon quite a few of the attributes which could be ascribed to all four nationalities' and thus it is implied that at this stage collective national or 'consensual' stereotyping of foreigners emerges. The authors also claim that there may be a discernible order in the stages whereby children acquire 'nationality concepts'. The first step is the acquisition of an affective stance. 'In the absence of factual knowledge, they search for available cues which differentiate various groups of people' (p. 358). In the second phase the child acquires information about the 'physical characteristics, customs and habits and general traits' whilst the 'affective response remains relatively constant':

> At the same time, the child becomes increasingly aware that individual variation must exist amongst the people who fall into these various groups, leading him or her to regard the attributes which have been acquired as merely characteristic rather than defining. Thus, at the end of this process, the child will have acquired, for each nationality, both a cluster of descriptive attributes and a generalized affective response. (Barret and Short, 1992, p. 358)

While many of the findings complement the results of the CRMLE study which will be described later in this chapter, the two research projects differ at least in one important respect. The analysis of the 'nationality concepts' (or stereotypes, to use a more common term) conducted by the developmental psychologists referred to above inevitably focuses on the conceptualization of the *differences* between European peoples and cultures whereas the focus of studies, including our own, of European awareness and identity is on an attempt to define the extent of existing and potential *unifying* conceptions. The two, however, may be obverse sides of the same coin and further research needs to be done to establish more clearly the relationship between attitudes which stress difference and those which express solidarity.

The authors of the present study decided to incorporate the first and third approaches in the planning of the research project and in the design of the pupil questionnaire. But before examining the CRMLE findings it is worth considering one further approach of study in this area as represented in the body of empirical research carried out by social psychologists.

Social psychological studies of attitudes towards Europe

Robert Baron and Donn Byrne (1981) define the discipline of social psychology as 'the scientific field that studies the manner in which the behaviour, feelings, or thoughts of the individual are influenced or determined by the behaviour and/or characteristics of others' (p. 7). In recent years some social psychologists have found the question of the determining influences behind young people's attitudes towards Europe a fertile field of enquiry, and at least three major empirical studies have been conducted which are worthy of note in the context of our own objectives. Miles Hewstone (1986, pp. 9–12) offers an illuminating overview of studies in this area relating them to different theories of integration. He describes four main theoretical approaches to identifying European integration: federalist (which emphasizes the 'legalistic perspective on sovereignty, and … the transfer of formal power from national to supra-national bodies'); pluralist (which holds that 'the development of a popular consensus towards the new institutions is a prerequisite for integration'); functionalist (which 'views ties of mutual affection, identity and loyalty as the building-blocks of integration'); and neo-functionalist (which is concerned with identifying the 'determinants of integration'). An early authoritative example of the fourth approach is the research conducted by Ronald Inglehart in the 1970s. Inglehart carried out a number of cross-national surveys on social and political attitudes and sought to identify the sources and consequences of the interaction between 'system-level' and 'individual-level' change. He argued, for instance, that improved economic conditions and the absence of 'total' war during the past generation led to an 'increasing emphasis on needs for belonging, esteem and self-realization' which in turn brought about 'system-level' change through the rise of 'élite-challenging issue-oriented groups' and the rise of supra-national loyalties (Inglehart, 1977, p. 5). He also concluded that support for European integration is influenced by 'a process of intergenerational change' (Inglehart and Reif, 1991, p. 11) which is partly accounted for by a shift from Materialist value priorities ('giving priority to physical sustenance and safety') to Postmaterialist value priorities (with a 'heavier emphasis on belonging, self-expression and the quality of life'). In his 1973 survey, a higher percentage of 15 to 24-year-olds named 'Europe' or 'the world as a whole' as either first or second choice as the 'geographical unit I belong to first of all' (p. 12).

Hewstone's own empirical research involved surveying by questionnaire 545 university students (mainly from the social sciences, but also including arts and natural science students). The students, aged between 20 and 22, were from West Germany, Italy, France and the UK. As well as partly following in the 'neo-functionalist' tradition, Hewstone relates his approach to the theory of 'social representation' formulated by Serge Moscovici: 'By social representations we mean a set of concepts, statements and explanations originating in daily life in the course of inter-individual communication' (Moscovici, 1981, p. 181). The object of enquiry here is the way in which mass society assimilates specialist knowledge and ideas, relates them to existing schemata and represents them through the medium of common sense discourse. Through his research study Hewstone sought to analyse this process by developing and testing 'an explanatory model of European attitudes' (1986, p. 88). His questionnaire asked respondents to evaluate political and economic goals of the EC, and to comment on the probability of achieving them, to rate achievements of common EC policy, to comment on gains and losses on specific economic issues, to comment on relations with independent countries, to ascribe and evaluate characteristics to nationalities and countries. Open-ended questioning allowed him to look for evidence of consensual representation amongst his sample. Hewstone acknowledges, however, that since his study focuses exclusively on the views of university students (who can be categorized as the 'educational élite of their generation') his data cannot be said to represent the European attitudes of a wide spectrum of the population.

A third empirical study in this vein is that of Adrian Furnham and Barrie Gunter who carried out a series of four surveys of 2000 UK adolescents, aged between 12 and 22 years. The aim of this project was to investigate the social attitudes of British adolescents over a broad range of issues, one of which being the adolescents' knowledge of and attitudes to the EEC. The latter were grouped in economic, cultural and political sections. The authors concluded that British adolescents' attitudes towards the EEC were equivocal: while on the whole the EEC was seen as successful economically and culturally, there was 'considerable hesitancy' over losing sovereignty to a European parliament. In terms of methodology the main additional value incorporated in this study is that the surveys were conducted in four separate 'waves' and that therefore the attitudes gathered reflect a totality of views expressed over time.

The insights provided by the social psychological studies summarized above and the theoretical analyses elaborated by that discipline are clearly of great value to an educational analysis of pupils' views on Europe and the influences which determine their attitudes. Specific points of comparison with the CRMLE study will be made in the exposition below. However, what sets educational research apart from social psychological research in this area is precisely the educational context. None of the researchers mentioned above considers in detail the role that schools play in forming children's perceptions. Furnham and Gunter, for instance, recruited their respondents through the National Association of Youth Clubs.

SUMMARY OF THE CRMLE RESEARCH PROJECT

In all, the research project undertaken by the authors of this book surveyed 1337 pupils in 25 secondary schools in England, France, Germany, Italy, the Netherlands and Spain. The schools were situated in Evreux and Ensisheim (France), Bielefeld, Darmstadt and Hanover (Germany), Castrovillari, Cosenza and Milan (Italy), Leek and Groningen (Netherlands), Granada, Oviedo and Salamanca (Spain). The largest sample was taken from schools in England. These were not chosen randomly but according to two criteria: first, in order to ensure a cross-section of the types of school currently in existence (inner city comprehensive, rural comprehensive, voluntary aided, grant maintained, grammar, city technology college and independent). The schools were located in Cambridgeshire, Coventry, Derby, Leeds, Nottingham, Reading, Rochdale, Stafford and Upton. The second criterion relating to the choice of English schools was that they were known personally to the authors, thereby ensuring a positive reception from staff and senior management. The European mainland schools also covered a range of types of school from a variety of social and geographical areas. In each school, two classes of Year 10 pupils (or their equivalent in mainland Europe) were surveyed. As a whole, the groups spanned the ability range.

The main instrument for data collection was a pupil questionnaire (see Appendix A1) which was first compiled in English and later translated (and marginally adjusted in order to obtain equivalent cross-national information) into the languages of the other countries involved. The questionnaire was appended by a brief true or false quiz consisting of twenty statements about Europe or European issues including historical, political, geographical, economic and legal topics. In this way, the main focus of the project, which was pupils' perceptions of their knowledge and attitudes towards Europe, could be set against some evidence of the extent of their actual European knowledge.

It was decided to adopt an open interpretation of the notion of Europe. Though the pupils surveyed would be members of the European Union, the opinions and attitudes we sought would also relate to other European countries which at the time were not members of the EU. Identification with Europe is not synonymous with identification with the European Union as an institution. The latter might in the present historical circumstances be a likely outcome of the former but should not form the starting-point of an investigation of this kind. Many pupils had thoughts and feelings about their European-ness while knowing very little indeed about the EU.

A number of political or European events formed a backcloth to the project. In July 1993 the UK government was defeated in the House of Commons during the Maastricht debate. In 1994 the debate focused on monetary union and on the enlargement of the EU to include Austria, Sweden, Finland and Norway. Silvio Berlusconi won the legislative elections in Italy following unprecedented corruption scandals involving the previous administration. Elections were also held for the newly enlarged European parliament in June 1994. In the UK (as in mainland Europe) there were many special anniversaries of the Second World War, the most prominent being the commemoration of D-Day (itself a source of some controversy in France and England). Meanwhile, the war in Bosnia continued. Less momentous but economically significant events took place, such as the opening of the Channel Tunnel in May and BMW's takeover of the UK Rover group. While it would be unwise to suggest that all the pupils we surveyed were aware of the European import of these issues, some information (albeit often heavily slanted) will have filtered through to them as a result of intense media coverage.

It should be stated at the outset that the relatively restricted size of our sample does not allow us to claim with certainty that our findings are representative of the attitudes and perceptions of the majority of young people in Europe. The analysis and conclusions we draw primarily reflect the views expressed by the pupils we surveyed *at a given moment in time*. The picture we can draw amounts to a snapshot which can be placed alongside the few others which have now been taken. There is a need for further extensive research to update our understanding of how young people relate to Europe. In the meantime, however, we can begin by looking at the evidence that is available.

Pupils' perceptions of their own knowledge about Europe

Overall, 54.7 per cent of the respondents to the questionnaire felt 'quite well informed' about Europe, with a further 2.8 per cent who felt 'very well informed' (see Table B3.1 in Appendix B). In their view, the main sources of their knowledge were the media (54.8 per cent said most or all of their knowledge was gained from this source) and school (46.5 per cent). Family was seen by a relatively small number as a source of information about Europe (27.4 per cent). There was a wider spread of responses to the question of how often they learned about Europe in school. 36.6 per cent said a few lessons a week, and 9.9 per cent said 'never or almost never' (see Table B3.9 in Appendix B). The subjects from which they felt they gained either some or a lot of their knowledge were geography (78.7 per cent), history (68.5 per cent) and modern languages (60 per cent). Other surveys (Bordas and Giles Jones, 1993; Goodson and McGivney, 1985; and Patterson and Sahni, 1994) would seem to confirm that in the eyes of pupils these three 'traditional' subjects continue to serve as the main vehicles for the promotion of the European dimension in schools rather than subjects such as civics, social studies and politics. Non-humanities subjects such as the sciences apparently remain divorced from the issue.

Some indications of factual knowledge

The respondents' overall lack of confidence in their knowledge and understanding of European matters was to some extent reflected in the answers they gave to a twenty-statement quiz which accompanied the survey questionnaire and was completed under the same conditions. Once again, it would be foolish to rush into wild generalizations on the basis of a slim test such as this, but it is useful to place the attitudes and perceptions in some context of factual knowledge. The statements were selected in part to indicate general knowledge about Europe as a continent, and in part about current EU policies which might affect their lives more directly than others (see Appendix A1). The mean score for the test was eleven. Out of the 1337 respondents, the highest score was reached by one pupil who obtained nineteen correct answers out of twenty, and at the other end of the scale there were fourteen pupils who scored nil. The statements for which there was more than a 60 per cent overall correct score were:

- 'There are twelve member states of the EC' (80 per cent correct)
- 'The Fall of the Berlin wall signified the end of the Second World War' (77 per cent correct)
- 'The Greek currency is called the bouzouki' (71.2 per cent correct)
- 'Luxembourg is the name of a city' (68.9 per cent correct)
- 'Belgium, Denmark, Holland, Spain and the UK are monarchies' (68.4 per cent correct)
- 'Dutch is one of three official languages spoken in Belgium' (67.5 per cent correct)
- 'The European Central Bank will be situated in Frankfurt, Germany' (63.7 per cent correct)
- 'The EC has the ultimate say on issues regarding road safety' (60.7 per cent correct)

As can be seen, most of the statements answered correctly by the majority of pupils were about general knowledge. On the other hand, the lowest scores related to statements about current EU policy:

- 'It is an EC regulation that all pupils must learn at least one foreign language at school' (15.9 per cent correct)
- 'A Briton who wants to work in France for longer than a year has to obtain a work permit' (24.2 per cent correct)
- 'The UK cannot send troops to fight in a war zone (e.g. Bosnia) without the consent of the European Parliament' (29.9 per cent correct)
- 'The EC intends to introduce a common system of school examinations for all member states' (34.9 per cent correct)

From this evidence it would appear that teenagers have little accurate knowledge about the European Union. The perceived reliance on the media as the main source of information might mean that certain more sensational events or issues are encountered by the young, but the more practical, less contentious and therefore probably more durable decisions pass them by. Teachers introduce their pupils to the historical, geographical, linguistic and cultural facets of Europe, but the social and economic developments of the European Union remain largely untouched. As a consequence, young people are likely to have either an exaggerated or a confused vision of what the European Union can do and is doing.

Pupils' unstructured statements about reasons for interest in Europe

When asked if they would like to know and understand more about Europe, those who responded positively gave reasons for their answers under nine broad categories:

(1) Work

I'd like to know more so that I'd be better prepared regarding work in Europe and also be able to compare the Italian situation with the European one. (Italian)

If I wanted to work in Europe I would want to know about it beforehand. (English)

Having a greater knowledge of Europe would help me in the business world when I get older. (English)

(2) Information and knowledge

There was a general dissatisfaction expressed from all the countries over the amount of information about Europe being made available to them.

I feel that we don't get enough information from school and that it could be far better taught. (German)

I want to be better informed about what is happening outside my country. (Italian)

Knowledge is the basis of all development. (Italian)

I would like to know more about Europe because it helps you to understand what is happening in the news and so you know which countries belong to Europe. (English)

We are not well enough informed. They need to make at least one TV channel about Europe or a European newspaper. (French)

Because a lot happens in Europe. Because as I watch TV I don't understand anything. (French)

(3) Personal interest

I'd like to know more for personal interest because we live in Europe. (Italian)

It gets a bit boring just knowing about your own country. If you go abroad you will know more about the country you are going to and it will be more enjoyable. (English)

Because my hobby is motorcross and I would like to know about motorcross in Europe. (English)

(4) Travel

This was a popular reason for valuing learning about Europe. It dominated the English responses in particular, which also contained comparatively fewer political statements and often expressed a tourist interest in mainland Europe.

I like to travel. (Italian)

I like to know about Europe so that I can travel. I would know what to expect when I go into another country. (French)

I love travelling and visiting other countries. Knowledge about these countries will always come in useful some time in my travels/life. (English)

(5) Communication and understanding

Comments in this vein indicated an openness to cultural variety and mutual understanding.

It would be nice to know it more in depth and communicate with other people. (Italian)

I think that it is important for teenagers and children to learn about Europe while they are quite young so they can understand about other people's cultures and their way of living. (English)

Very little information about Europe is given in school. I think it would be beneficial for the future of Europe if children understood more about it. (English)

I'd like to know people from other countries. (Spanish)

I'd be able to understand the problems better. (Spanish)

It [European matters] *sounds interesting and I would like to understand it a bit more.* (English)

(6) Language learning

Where this was explicitly referred to it was generally associated with cultural learning as well.

I would like to know how the different countries live. I would like to learn some other languages. (English)

(7) Citizenship

Many sophisticated political inferences were offered, primarily by the mainland Europeans. The attitude expressed in this category is often conative, justifying the interest by an intention to act or behave accordingly in the future as a result. The first two statements below are examples of this.

> *As a citizen of Europe I'd like to be better informed so as to act in the best way possible.* (Italian)

> *I would like to be well informed about Europe and Maastricht because later I will be a voter and for that it is necessary for me to have increased skills in order to vote properly.* (French)

> *Understanding each other better in Europe will lead to a greater overall understanding between countries.* (German)

> *I feel we have too little information to make judgements. I would like to know much more about politics and much less about geography.* (German)

> *Millions of people depend on the views of a few people. I would like to know who is making these decisions.* (Spanish)

> *We are getting closer and working together as a big union and helping each other and that's better.* (English)

> *To feel more of a participant in Europe.* (Italian)

> *It will make us more aware of our surroundings and we would feel we were more involved.* (English)

Their comments generally reveal a felt need for more pertinent information to help them form their own opinions and make responsible judgements for active citizenship.

(8) The Future

> *We are the 'new generation' and as adults we are going to live in this world. It's normal to want to know more about our future. We are badly informed about 'our' Europe which belongs to us all.* (French)

> *Because we mustn't face the future without the necessary resources.* (Italian)

> *So as to improve future conditions.* (Italian)

> *I think I'd like to know more about Europe because it is a place for the future which is extremely important for us all.* (English)

> *Because my social life is going to develop.* (Spanish)

(9) A sense of belonging

For some pupils the notion of belonging in Europe clearly had a strong appeal, often expressed through the use of the possessive pronoun 'my':

> *I live in a European country and would like to know more about my continent.* (Spanish)

> *It's the continent we live in.* (English)

> *We are part of Europe.* (English)

> *I belong in Europe.* (Spanish)

The following extract of an interview with a small group of English pupils casts an interesting light on the ways in which some adolescents 'anchor' (to borrow from Moscovici) their understanding of Europe within a familiar frame of reference:

'What is your personal attitude to the European Union?'

I think it is better that we are part of it. I think we should all get one currency, and even closer, even with Germany and Spain and Sweden.

I agree. Being an island we feel isolated, joining with other countries is better.

I agree. We are getting closer and working together as a big Union and helping each other and that's better.

We might get some good ideas from there – like machinery. Instead of competing with each other we might work together.

Eventually we'll be just one big happy family.

For this group, as with others, the appeal of the European Union is expressed in terms of integration (as opposed to the 'isolation' of being left out). Political closeness with Europe is 'objectified' (Moscovici, 1981, p. 192) in terms of physical links. We are isolated because we are an island and, as another pupil from a different English school put it: 'When the Channel Tunnel eventually opens I think we will be more connected to Europe and our connection will become stronger.' The pupils also express a combination of utilitarian support for European union (the UK will benefit by sharing technological information) and affective support (we'll help each other). Finally, the whole enterprise is recuperated by a metaphor which draws on a frame of reference familiar to all adolescents: 'we'll be just one big happy family'.

Negative statements

On the whole, negative statements about Europe were brief, neutrally phrased and with little qualification. In a few cases, a rational alternative was offered, such as interest in countries beyond Europe. On the whole, though, rejection of Europe seemed to go hand in hand with general disaffection.

I don't care. (English)

I'm not bothered one way or the other. (Spanish)

I am against Europe. (German)

I am not bothered to listen to rubbish about Europe. (English)

I am only 15 and I don't really see why we have to know anything about it till I'm older because I'm interested in a lot more other things, such as boys. (English)

I don't really want to know more. I'll get more information when I'm older. (English)

If I don't know much and I'm OK why should I want to learn more? (Spanish)

Looking over the open-ended comments as a whole, it may seem surprising that more than 1000 statements fall under a relatively limited range of topic headings. On the other hand, this would seem to suggest that an underlying consensus exists between European adolescents over priorities and perceptions of life ahead of them. Where differences occur, it would seem that the process of intellectual maturation may be playing a role. It is interesting to note, for instance, that many of the statements are egocentric (for example, 'I like to travel'). In these cases, justification of interest (or lack of interest) in Europe are related entirely to personal circumstances or desires. In other cases, more abstract and objective reasoning is put forward (for example, 'because there are problems which affect all countries'). It is noticeable that the negative statements were almost all egocentric.[1]

ANALYSIS OF QUANTITATIVE DATA

As was stated earlier, the CRMLE questionnaire was designed to prompt pupils' attitudes towards Europe both directly and indirectly. The direct, global (or 'diffuse' in the social psychologists' jargon) expression of views on Europe was elicited through, for instance, the question relating to identity. Overall, in reply to the question 'Do you think of yourself as European?' 43.9 per cent of respondents answered 'yes, totally', 34.3 per cent 'only partly' and 21.7 per cent 'not at all'. One must interpret this statistic with caution. Pro-European commentators might take some comfort in the numerically greater response made by the pupils expressing total or partial European identity over those who rejected this identity totally. However, one should also pay special attention to the middle category, 'only partly', selected by a third of the sample. The word 'only' marks a certain reserve which many of the pupils found appropriate to their feelings. Clearly, the responses to this question reveal that there are degrees of affective attachment to Europe which may play some part in influencing their attitudes on specific, utilitarian issues. A more unambiguously positive stance is found in the responses to the question: 'Would you like to know and understand more about Europe?' 5.3 per cent said 'no', 27.4 per cent said they were 'not bothered' and 67.4 per cent said 'yes'.

However, general statements alone do not give a clear picture of the nature of the attitudes they seek to define. In what sense do the teenagers think of themselves as Europeans: geographically, historically, culturally, ethnically, politically? Indeed it is probable that one person's attachment to the idea of Europe will not remain constant when considered through these different perspectives. In order to sharpen the focus of our research, the survey first asked the teenagers to place a range of socio-political issues in order of priority and secondly to state whether policy decisions should be made at national, EC, or both national and EC levels. The issues in question were: defence, employment, immigration, pollution, health education, crime, drugs, equal opportunities, race relations, Bosnia, the third world, the family, justice and terrorism. In this way, it was hoped to achieve a more detailed critical analysis of the way teenagers think about socio-political issues and about the corresponding responsibilities of EU and national governments. A further benefit from this approach was that one might be able to infer a clearer view of the boundaries of pupils' current attachment to Europe. A number of significant patterns emerge from which one can draw tentative conclusions.

How do teenagers' views on Europe compare with those of adults?

Table 2.1 is a summary of the overall response to the question about where policy decision-making should take place on specific issues.

Table 2.1 *Percentages of total responses to the question: 'Do you think that the following issues should be dealt with by the national government or by the European Community?'*

Issue	EC level	National level	Both
Bosnia	85.4	10.9	3.7
The Third World	84.6	10.3	5.1
Race relations	68.7	26.6	4.8
Immigration	67.3	30.7	1.5
Drugs	61.2	33.9	3.9
Equal opportunities	58.3	36.4	3.8
Pollution	56	40	4
Terrorism	54.2	39.5	4.8
Defence	46.4	47.3	1.9
Crime	38.9	57	4.1
Health education	35.1	62.1	2.8
Justice	32.5	63.4	4.1
Employment	25.5	72.3	2.2
The family	16.6	80.1	3.1

It is interesting to compare these figures with a survey of 1000 people per member state carried out on behalf of the European Commission prior to the June 1994 European elections and therefore conducted at almost the same time as our own CRMLE research. A similar question concerning the role of national and EU government on specific socio-political issues yielded the information given in Table 2.2 (European Commission, 1994).

Table 2.2 *Percentage of total responses to the question: 'Do you think that the following issues should be dealt with by the British [French etc.] government or by the European Community?'*

Issues	EC level	National level
Third World cooperation	75	17
Drugs	71	25
Foreign policy	68	22
Environment	64	31
Asylum	55	38
Immigration	54	40
Unemployment	52	44
Defence	50	45
Health	31	64
Education	30	65

The attitudes of youth and adulthood seem to concur on the relative roles of the two levels of government over many issues. A high EU score appears in both age groups on the Third World and foreign policy matters. Also, approximately equivalent scores are made for drugs, the environment, immigration, defence and health. A significant divergence between the two surveys, however, can be found with regard to the issue of unemployment. Of the adults surveyed, 52 per cent thought that the issue needed to be dealt with at EU level, whereas only 25.5 per cent of the teenagers surveyed thought it was a matter for the EC. The difference might be partly accounted for by the fact that in the *Eurobarometer* survey the issue is referred to as 'unemployment' and in the CRMLE survey as 'employment'. In the former case, the wording may suggest a negative status quo which is beyond the power or means of the national government to redress and for which the EU might be seen as a source of positive intervention. The term 'employment' on the other hand, is positive and therefore more likely to appeal to feelings of national self-reliance. A different interpretation of the divergence here is that the imminence of employment or unemployment is more pressing for all 14 to 16-year-olds than it is for the full adult age range and that consequently, because of its importance, the younger age group are more likely to think the issue should be dealt with nationally.

Other indications of overall similarity of attitudes between the generations are that in both surveys the most pro-European country seems to be the Netherlands. 77 per cent of Dutch people think membership of the EU is a 'good thing' and 70 per cent believe that their country has benefited from EU membership (*Eurobarometer* survey). 90.4 per cent of Dutch teenagers questioned in the CRMLE survey think of themselves as European. At the other end of the scale, only 42 per cent of UK adults think their country has benefited from membership (*Eurobarometer* survey). Similarly, the English teenagers' response was the lowest: only 18.6 per cent think of themselves as totally European, 41.6 per cent as partly European and 39.8 per cent as not at all European (this last figure being significantly higher than any of the other nationalities represented in the survey, as shown in Table 2.5).

Which factors appear to have most influence over teenagers' views on Europe?

Gender

The most striking feature of the overall pattern of responses to the questionnaire is the gender difference in attitudes to Europe. While on the question of national identity there was an even balance between males and females (74.7 per cent and 75.2 per cent respectively felt totally British or French etc.), on the matter of European identity 47.3 per cent of females considered themselves totally European as against 40.5 per cent of the male respondents (in other words a difference of 6.8 per cent). Similarly, on most issues more females than males think that decisions should be made at an EC rather than a national level. The topics where the difference is greatest are immigration (10.3 per cent), justice (8.3 per cent), drugs (5.2 per cent) and equal opportunities (4.5 per cent). On the male side, there were only two issues on which there was a significantly larger percentage of pro-European responses: pollution (2.1 per cent) and health education (4.9 per cent). The relative pro-European female stance is repeated in each of the countries represented.

This gender difference, however, is reversed in the adult survey reported in the *Eurobarometer* (June 1993). Other surveys also show women to be less enthusiastic than men on Europe. Writers suggest that this may be partly due to a general lack of interest or confidence in political matters: as indicated by a higher percentage of female 'don't knows' and lack of replies to a 1983 survey. The age factor, too, is significant: 34 per cent of women over 55 say they are 'not at all interested in EC' as opposed to 29 per cent of women aged 15 to 24, according to the same poll (see Mossuz-Lavau, 1991). The more positive attitude of youth, with a greater open-mindedness and acceptance of new ideas for the future, seems to express itself more readily through the European attitudes of young women. Furnham and Gunter (1989, p. 72) also found that among the students they surveyed, the females 'tended to be less distrustful of the EEC, less chauvinistic and patriotic, and more in favour of closer union [with Europe]'. This is a reality which planners and promoters of the European dimension in schools would do well to bear in mind.

Class

The pattern of responses also indicates some influence of social factors in the way teenagers think about Europe. Of those whose parents were social class D, 44.9 per cent considered themselves as 'not at all European'. They were also more likely to see national government as the place for policy decision-making. On eleven out of fourteen issues it was this social category which registered the lowest European score. There was no equivalent indication at the positive end of the scale. Highest European scores here were more or less evenly distributed between youngsters from social class A families (4 issues), social class B families (4 issues) and social class D families (5 issues), with social class C1 families (1 issue). But the percentage differences were in many cases statistically insignificant.

Travel: 'Europe through Europe'

The variable of whether or not the respondents had visited another European country did seem to have some effect on their attitude to decision-making on issues. On nine issues those who had visited other countries registered a pro-European stance; on two issues there was no marked difference; but on crime, family and health education those who had not travelled to other European countries registered a higher European score. The suggestion that 'notions of "us" and "them" can become stronger as a result of more travel' (Macdonald, 1993) is not borne out by the evidence of our findings. Travel seems also to be a factor in influencing a sense of European identity. Of those who had not been to another European country, 26.4 per cent felt 'not at all European' as opposed to 20 per cent of those who had been. However, one can argue that those teenagers who choose to travel are in all likelihood more favourably disposed to Europe and foreignness in general and that consequently their pro-European stance is predictable.

Pupils' conscious perception of the influence of travel on their acquisition of knowledge about Europe can be gauged from the fact that of those who had been to another European country, 20 per cent said that they had gained no information about Europe from the experience, 51.6 per cent had gained a little, 26.1 per cent had gained most of their information from this source and 2.3 per cent said that they had acquired all their information from travel. Of course, pupils may learn informally through travel in a multitude of ways without them consciously recognizing the experience as a cognitive gain. But their perception of the effect on their knowledge might indicate the extent to which teachers draw pupils' attention to the wider European context of visits to individual countries. It would appear that in most cases this is often a missed opportunity. From our data, it would seem that youngsters from the northern European countries have greater opportunities to travel within Europe than others (see Table 2.3).

Table 2.3   *Breakdown by country of response to the question: 'Have you ever travelled to another European country?'*

	England	France	Spain	Germany	Italy	Netherlands	Total
Travelled	407	156	86	161	78	112	1000
	73.9%	86.7%	50.6%	92%	55.7%	95.7%	74.8%
Not	144	24	84	14	62	5	333
travelled	26.1%	13.3%	49.4%	8%	44.3%	4.3%	25%

Economic considerations would also seem, not surprisingly, to determine the frequency of travel. The largest social class groupings of pupils who had not travelled abroad were those whose parents were class D (41.1 per cent) or unemployed (54 per cent).

What role are schools playing in promoting 'Europe through Europe'? Just over half of the total sample (51.9 per cent) said they had not travelled to another European country with their school. Once again a pattern emerges, showing more pupils from the northern countries travelling with their school than pupils from the southern countries. Furthermore, pupils at English schools travel more often with their school than their counterparts on the mainland. For instance, at an independent school in Yorkshire, three of the pupils surveyed had travelled nine times to Europe with their school; 75.2 per cent of those surveyed at the school had been twice or more with the school. This phenomenon is not restricted to wealthy independent schools. Two pupils from our sample at a Roman Catholic high school in the Midlands had been to Europe nine times with the school, and 48 per cent had been twice or more. Similarly, two pupils from our sample at a Cambridgeshire village college had been seven times with their school and 55 per cent had been twice or more. At the other end of the scale, none of the pupils we surveyed at one Italian school had been to another European country with their school. Similarly, Spanish pupils had little experience of travel abroad through this channel. In each of the three Spanish schools surveyed, about half of the pupils in our sample had not travelled at all within Europe with their school (see Table B2.7 in Appendix B).

There is scant evidence from our research that schools in Europe are compensating for the financial restraints on travel felt in particular by the pupils from poorer families. Only a very small percentage of those who had travelled with school had parents who were unemployed (2 per cent) or social class D (4.6 per cent).

Ethnic origin

This too seems to play a significant role in shaping the teenagers' attitudes towards Europe (see Table 2.4).

Table 2.4 *Breakdown by ethnic origin of total responses to the question: 'Do you think of yourself as European?'*

	Afro-Caribbean	Asian	White	Other
Not at all	55%	46.5%	20.2%	9.8%
Only partly	40%	43.4%	31.8%	46.2%
Yes, totally	5%	10.1%	47.9%	43.9%

Perhaps unsurprisingly, a much greater proportion of 'white' teenagers accept a European identity than do those from ethnic minority backgrounds. Clearly, Afro-Caribbeans and Asians living in Europe already have a dual identity and belong to two cultures. The idea of totally assuming a third European identity is not likely to be popular. However, the figures show that a slightly larger proportion of Afro-Caribbeans and Asians feel they are partly European than do whites. Again this could be explained by the fact that ethnic minority groups are more at home with the idea of multinational identity and of coming to terms with accommodating their parents' cultures and backgrounds with those of the home country of which they are citizens.

If we look specifically at the responses of pupils from England (see Tables B7.12 and B7.13 in Appendix B), we find that the responses to the questions 'Do you consider yourself European?' and 'Do you consider yourself British?' reveal that a larger proportion of Asians than of whites do not consider themselves at all European (though the numbers are relatively high in both cases). Approximately the same figures are registered for the 'only partly European' response (45.5 per cent Asian and 39.9 per cent whites). The difference between the ethnic groupings is much greater in relation to national identity. 57.7 per cent of Asians felt 'only partly British' as opposed to only 18.6 per cent of whites. For many of the Asians we surveyed, therefore, the ambiguity and complexity of their feelings of cultural allegiance relate both to Europe and to the UK. Of the 554 pupils we surveyed in England, thirteen said they considered themselves 'not at all European' *and* 'not at all British'. This group included five whites and five Asians.

The ambiguities appear even deeper on observing that, of the 386 pupils in English schools who said they were 'totally British', 134 also felt 'only partly European' and 85 felt 'totally European'. Of the latter, four were of Asian descent. What does it mean to be 'totally' British and European? It would seem that in the eyes of youngsters the notion of total identification has a lateral and a depth dimension. For some, to claim total allegiance to Europe, or their nation state, would imply exclusion of other possible cultural ties, including their ethnicity. For others, total allegiance to Europe simply indicates the depth of their attachment to their future within Europe. Cultural identities are notoriously difficult to define when viewed from within; but from an external point of view differences melt away. In the UK, the Asian community comprises a range of different religious, linguistic and ethnic backgrounds. Yet when compared with a non-Asian community, a unifying identity emerges. Similarly, a British identity emerges in contrast with, say, a French one and a European identity emerges in opposition with, for example, an American identity. In *England My England*, George Orwell points to the same shifting perspective in cultural identities:

> It is quite true that the so-called races of Britain feel themselves to be very different from one another. A Scotsman, for instance, does not thank you if you call him an Englishman. You can see the hesitation we feel on this point by the fact that we call our islands by no

less than six different names, England, Britain, Great Britain, the British Isles, the United Kingdom and, in very exalted moments, Albion. Even the differences between north and south England loom large in our own eyes. But somehow these differences fade away the moment that any two Britons are confronted by a European. It is very rare to meet a foreigner, other than an American, who can distinguish between English and Scots or even English and Irish. To a Frenchman, the Breton and the Auvergnat seem very different beings, and the accent of Marseilles is a stock joke in Paris. Yet we speak of 'France' and 'the French', recognizing France as an entity, a single civilization, which in fact it is. So also with ourselves. Looked at from the outside, even the Cockney and the Yorkshireman have a strong resemblance.[2]

It would seem that youngsters also operate these different levels of cultural identification.

Nationality

Direct responses to the question of European identity produced a significant divergence between English (and to a lesser extent French) pupils and those of the other four countries, as shown in Table 2.5.[3]

Table 2.5   *Breakdown by country of total responses to the question: 'Do you think of yourself as European?'*

	Not at all %	Only partly %	Yes, totally %
England	39.8	41.6	18.6
France	17.4	41	41.6
Germany	10.5	26.3	62.6
Italy	4.3	41	54.7
Netherlands	2.6	7	90.4
Spain	6.4	25.1	68.4

Elsewhere in the questionnaire the notion of 'European unity' was placed more discreetly among a list of other important social and political issues. An analysis of variance applied to the pupils' responses to this question, asking them to select and place in order of importance the ten most pressing issues in their own country, shows that a higher rating was given to the issue of European unity by Spain and Italy, a higher rating for pollution by the north European countries (especially the Netherlands), and a higher rating given to the issue of corruption by Italy. In all these cases it can be assumed that teenagers reflect the dominant concerns of their country particularly as represented by their respective media.

On the question of where decision-making should occur, the French responses scored the top pro-EU ratings on six, mainly social, issues; the Germans gave the highest EU rating for justice, terrorism and defence (with Italy giving the lowest EU score in each of these); and the Italians gave the largest national pro-European vote on the foreign affairs issues of Bosnia and the Third World, as well as on race relations. The English yielded the lowest pro-European count in five cases.

It is also worth noting that except for race relations and immigration, a higher percentage of Spanish teenagers thought that decisions should be made at both national and EU levels for every issue mentioned. While the figures involved are low, the pattern invites some consideration. Could it be that, with the newly established autonomous regions in Spain, the Spanish people are more adapted to thinking of government operating at both central and regional levels?

When asked for their views on changes which have already happened or may happen as a result of closer European unity, an interesting reversal occurs in pro- and anti-European stances in some cases (see Table 2.6).

Table 2.6   *Highest percentage scores in each category. For a full national breakdown of these responses, see Table B6.2 in Appendix B.*

Change	In favour %	Not bothered %	Against %
The national currency is replaced by the ECU	Italy 83.6 Total 38.5	Spain 38.2 Total 27.5	Germany 47.7 England 45.9 Total 34
More decisions affecting your life are taken in Strasbourg	France 30.3 Italy 30.2 Total 14.3	Germany 62 Total 38.7	Netherlands 65.8 Total 46.9
Working without restriction in EU member states	Italy 88.6 Total 59.1	England 35.6 Total 23.7	Netherlands 23.9 Total 17
EU citizens able to vote in country of residence regardless of nationality	Italy 70 Total 54	England 32.9 Total 23.8	France 27 Netherlands 28.2 Total 22
Greater uniformity of education and training	Italy 94.2 Total 60.7	England 43.6 Total 31.5	Netherlands 24.8 Total 7.5

Although there was no majority from any country in favour of the general idea of more decision-making taking place in Strasbourg rather than in the national parliament, there was, on the other hand, a majority in every country represented apart from England (who scored 48.4 per cent) favouring greater uniformity of education and training across member states. When read alongside the pupils' answers to the education statements in the quiz (see earlier discussion in this chapter), one can conclude that European teenagers think that there is more planned educational harmonization with the EU than is the case, and that the teenagers would on the whole welcome such a move.

As a further example of the indeterminate nature of the attitudes held on Europe, it is worth noting that while the Dutch respondents expressed very strong pro-European views elsewhere in the questionnaire (and in particular in global terms), in this section they registered the highest negative vote in four out of five cases. Conversely, the Italian respondents, who in general terms did not express a markedly pro-European stance, registered the highest pro-European vote in four of the five questions in this section, almost equalling the top score registered by the French in the fifth statement which deals with the expansion of the role of Strasbourg.

THE EUROPEAN DIMENSION *FOR* EUROPE

What role do schools play in shaping these views on change in the European scene? In order to find any traces of education acting as a catalyst for the creation of a future

Europe we have to look to the interview data. Even so, what scant evidence there is of educating for European citizenship is found not at the national, organized level but at best at the individual school level, if not at the individual teacher level. No doubt this reticence of national governments to give a lead is influenced by educators' inability to define what education for citizenship is and it is bolstered by the abuse of subsidiarity as an excuse for avoiding change. It is quite clear from teacher and pupil interviews that what few initiatives there are in responding to the call for a European dimension in education, they are initiatives associated much more with the development of awareness than citizenship. In only one instance was there evidence of a school having elements of a European dimension directly expressed in its mission aims. Moreover there is still an underlying anxiety about teaching for European citizenship. One English teacher in a senior position remarked: 'I think that in any issues that are controversial if you give a personal view, I don't see a problem as long as it is obvious that it is a personal view.'

But given that pupils are *de facto* citizens of Europe, why should it be controversial to teach about their rights and obligations as citizens not only at the national level but also at the regional and European? It does not lie within the scope of this chapter to attempt an answer to that question. This will be discussed in Chapter 4. However, empirical data does demonstrate that it is precisely the lack of a coherent national impetus that is preventing an Education *for* Europe. Teachers in France, while recognizing that citizenship was part of the prescribed curriculum, were well aware that this aspect could, in reality, be ignored. While expecting to see as outcomes from the European dimension in the curriculum (in the shape of *éducation civique*), more understanding, less narrow-mindedness and an awareness that pupils might be able to get a job abroad, the influence in reality that the school had was not extensive. One French teacher claimed that 'the perceptions of Europe are limited by the pupils' ability to travel', again suggesting that school itself was not really compensating for the personal circumstances of particular social groups.

Italian teachers bemoaned the inertia and lack of directive from central government, having to resort to personal initiatives largely financed out of their own pockets. English teachers, overwhelmed by educational change, had placed the European dimension (let alone educating for European citizenship) quite firmly at the bottom of the list of priorities. Even among teachers (like this German teacher of English who felt that Europe was integrated quite normally into their language teaching) there was a feeling that so far this had been *about* rather than *for*: 'I should like to see more openness amongst the pupils to questions about Europe. They must have a dream if they are to make progress.'

The interview data revealed one further important factor which no doubt determines how the European dimension is viewed and taught in schools. Virtually none of the teachers interviewed had been on an in-service training course directly linked to the introduction of the European dimension in schools. Nor was there any special provision made in terms of special resources in order to promote the European dimension. Teachers in general were much more cynical about the amount of European dimension teaching that went on in their school than headteachers were.

It is not surprising, therefore, that when pupils were asked if they could remember doing anything about Europe, any recollection of such an event in a lesson was always *about* (usually in the humanities) or *through* (language learning and school exchanges). There was not more than a handful of mentions (and two of these were as a result of autonomous projects, outside the school curriculum) of work directly related to European institutions, of work related to citizenship and of work related to the kinds of issues raised in the questionnaire. This lack of exploration of Europe as a political entity is all the more surprising when one considers, as we shall in the next two chapters, the positive nature of the responses obtained from headteachers and teachers to the current process of 'Europeanization'.

NOTES

1. Social psychologists have argued that political disaffection is associated with educational failure pre-16 (Brynner and Ashford, 1994). Poor educational performance is linked with a 'growing cynicism about politics' which leaves its mark in adulthood. This would seem to be *a fortiori* the case with regard to interest in European politics and citizenship.
2. George Orwell (1957) *Selected Essays* (Harmondsworth: Penguin), pp. 72–3.
3. In 1992, the *Guardian* newspaper reported on a Mintel survey which showed that 42 per cent of British adults and 53 per cent of 15–19-year-olds considered themselves 'European' (see Taylor, 1993). Our survey, taken three years later, would suggest a weaker identification with Europe on the part of English youth. An even bleaker finding was revealed in a Gallup poll of the British electorate carried out in February 1995, in which only 43 per cent thought Britain was part of Europe, and 57 per cent did not think of themselves as Europeans (see Waller, 1995).

Chapter 3

Implementing the European Dimension in Secondary Schools: Contexts and Issues

As a follow-up to the pupil questionnaires the research group was able to conduct a number of interviews with pupils and teachers in some of the schools that had taken part in the initial part of the project. The aim of this was to gain an understanding of the national contexts of the teaching and learning, and it was supported by an investigation into the curriculum requirements for the European dimension in the countries concerned. The interviews with the teachers raised issues relevant to them in their work of implementing national guidelines, such as in-service training, availability of materials, support in the school and beyond, educational reform and the context of the school in which they were working. It would appear from this evidence that there is a variety of emphases in the way that the European dimension is being implemented in the six countries of our study.

FRANCE

The national curriculum requirements of France contain compulsory sections about Europe and explicit references to the European Union. This would seem to stem from the French government's wish to prepare pupils for their responsibilities as citizens in national and international contexts. In the preface to the 1985 edition of the curriculum for the *collèges* (comprehensive schools for 11 to 15-year-olds) the then Minister of Education writes, 'J'ai eu la préoccupation d'assurer la formation des citoyens de demain' and, in summary, 'Il s'agit de construire une France forte, unie et solidaire par ses valeurs et par sa culture, une France ouverte et accueillante, capable de dialoguer avec les peuples et de coopérer avec les autres nations' (Chevènement, 1985).[1] There is an emphasis both on national heritage as well as on future developments in international cooperation. The commitment of France to the European dimension in the education of its young people has found expression in the national programmes of study and is in line with the traditional French policy of a centralized education system, dating back to the dictatorship of Napoleon and beyond.

In the *collèges* a considerable amount of time is allotted in the *classe de quatrième* and *classe de troisième* (13 to 14-year-olds and 14 to 15-year-olds) in history, geography and *éducation civique* (civic education) for the study of Europe in the twentieth century. In the schools in our research study the three subjects are taught by the same teacher in one block of curriculum time, using one of the published course books designed to fit the programmes of study. They state that in history the *classe de troisième* pupils work on the twentieth century right up to the present day. In geography the syllabus for the *classe de quatrième* begins by stating that the pupils in this year study the geography of Europe and requires the pupils to examine in detail the Benelux countries, Germany, the UK, Spain or Italy, an eastern European country and the European Union. *Education civique* requires a study also in the *classe de quatrième* of the institutions and functioning of the European Union, as well as its future development. By the time the pupils leave the *collège* they have gained from the humanities area of the curriculum considerable knowledge about Europe as well as of the political reality of the European Union.

The teachers of history, geography and *éducation civique* who were interviewed all spoke enthusiastically about the inclusion of the European dimension in their work, with one teacher in the school in Alsace expressing the view: 'I think that a teacher of history and geography can't be anything else other than European.' Any problems in their work which they mentioned in interview showed their wish to present the reality of the European Union and current events in Europe with up-to-date material. Many teachers thought that the text books were not up-dated regularly enough for them to keep up with current events, and reported using articles from newspapers and periodicals. There was a concern in the school in Normandy that history, geography and foreign languages are not enough to make the pupils sensitive to the European dimension, and a view that foreign travel is more important for knowledge of the everyday reality of life in another country. Again in Normandy one teacher spoke of the difficulty of explaining the work of the European Union to the pupils for whom Strasbourg and Brussels are so far away. Already the advantages of life in Alsace become apparent, placing the pupils and teachers at our target school in a privileged position because of their geographical situation.

The priority given in France to foreign language learning is high, English being by far the most popular, followed by German and Spanish. A large-scale initiative to promote foreign language learning in primary schools began in 1989 and has developed rapidly. In some *lycées* (schools for 15 to 18-year-olds) there is a 'European section' where foreign languages are the medium for teaching other subjects, and this is held in high regard. The basic requirement of the national curriculum is that all pupils begin a foreign language for three hours per week when they start secondary education and that a second foreign language can be chosen in extra time in the *classe de quatrième*. Almost all the pupils in our study (99.4 per cent) were learning two foreign languages. In the school in Alsace some pupils begin both English and German at the age of 11. This is regarded as very prestigious and the complications which this causes in the timetable arrangements are generally well accepted. In the school in Normandy, which is in an educational priority area (*Zone d'Education Prioritaire*), some pupils opt for extra lessons in their first foreign language in order to improve their performance, instead of taking the second foreign language. Both schools are making curriculum provision for the foreign language learning needs of their pupils in accordance with the national framework which stipulates continued study and provides no possibility for an opt-out. One foreign language is compulsory at the *lycées*, a second can be continued or started, and there is also the possibility of beginning a third.

All foreign language teachers interviewed supported the teaching of *civilisation*, by which they meant the inclusion of information about the societies where the target language is spoken, and they all stressed the need for school visits and exchanges to support their work. The course books for English used at both schools contain a wealth of material about British society. *Apple Pie*, for example, includes Red Nose Day, Childline and multinational Britain, encouraging a knowledge of the reality of the lives of many young people in England. The course books often also contain a section on the European Union as a peg on which to hang the teaching of the names of countries, languages and nationalities.

Looking beyond humanities and foreign languages, the French curriculum in the *collèges* offers an opportunity for the European dimension in the teaching of French. Foreign literature in translation may be studied, and texts by Agatha Christie as well as Russian texts were mentioned by one teacher in an interview. Apart from that much depended on individual teacher interests. At the school in Alsace a maths teacher interviewed said that she tried always to show that maths is an international subject and that there are different ways of working and of presentation. Another maths teacher spoke of his work over five years with pupils in a competition *maths sans frontières* where his class competed with classes in other countries. His personal commitment had involved him in a science and maths project with Germany to compare teaching programmes, the school German exchange programme and a school visit to Naples organized in collaboration with history and geography teachers. Other teachers mentioned school visits to Poland, Czechoslovakia, Austria and England, and a penfriend link with Greece. The teachers interviewed in Alsace all recognized the enormous advantage that they and their pupils had in being so close to the German and Swiss borders, in being able to watch television programmes in German and to go on weekly shopping trips to Germany as many of them did. In contrast, many of the teachers in the Normandy school spoke of the difficulties caused by the social make-up of the catchment area which create their own priorities in the school's development plan. In the Alsace school the European dimension had featured three years before our research on the school's development plan (*projet d'établissement*) and this had led to work with the Council of Europe. The deputy headteacher perceived the European dimension as being well established in the school. The headteacher in Normandy showed a great commitment to Europe which he hoped to realize in his school, particularly in the form of an extension of the exchange visits.

French pupils interviewed recognized the importance of school in the development of their knowledge about Europe. They considered themselves well informed and regarded school as a main source of information. In interviews they were able to point to other sources of information such as their own reading, the television and visits abroad. Their teachers had generally gained much experience of Europe through their own travel abroad, but none had been on any courses on the implementation of the European dimension in their subject area. Provision of such courses is the responsibility of the education region (*Académie*) and can vary in emphasis. Rouen, the regional centre for the Normandy school, and Strasbourg for the Alsace school both offered courses on Europe in their 1994/5 programmes, Strasbourg having a special Europe section in the publicity. One teacher of English at the school in Normandy had been on an international course in Sweden about course book provision and there had been a lecture about the European dimension in history and geography course books. This has helped to raise her awareness of the European dimension in her own area of the curriculum, but her priority was to find a suitable partnership school for penfriend links and an exchange visit.

France has recognized the need for local centres where resources for teaching and learning can be made available to teachers and has created for each *département* a *Centre National de Documentation Pédagogique* (CNDP). The centre in Normandy in the same town as our school contained a good deal of information about the European dimension, but generally there was a lack of help in providing practical ideas about lesson planning. This is recognized by Hopkins *et al.* (1994): 'we did not find evidence that in the case of the European dimension practical and imaginative support to schools, colleges and their staff is provided on anything approaching the scale of that offered by the Central Bureau/UKCEE'.

As a founder member of the European Union, France has shown a commitment to the European dimension in education through the curriculum, in contrast to England and Wales which have relied more on local initiatives and national support for extra-curricular activity. It has assured knowledge, but in the fostering of attitudes much will inevitably depend on the input of the teacher and the social context of the school.

GERMANY

Central to a consideration of the implementation of the European dimension in German schools is the document *Europa im Unterricht* ('Europe in the Classroom') published in 1978 by the Standing Conference for Education Ministers of the federal states (*Kultusministerkonferenz*, KMK) of what was then West Germany. This was the first attempt to determine how ideas and notions about Europe should be tackled in German schools. In 1983 *Entschließung zur Europapolitik*[2] showed the connection between work in schools about Europe and political development. The 1990 *Erlaß* (Decree) entitled *Europa im Unterricht* was written by the enlarged KMK after the reunification of Germany. It contains much rhetoric about the need to cultivate positive and responsible attitudes in the young, as their sense of European identity and citizenship is developed. Green (1995) identifies the central concept as 'Ziel der pädagogischen Arbeit muß es sein, in den jungen Menschen das Bewußtsein einer europäischen Identität zu erwecken'.[3]

The KMK has the function of harmonizing the work of the ministers of the sixteen *Länder* (federal states). It provides curriculum guidelines which are then interpreted in each state. The system stands in contrast to the centralized systems such as that of France, but again according to Green (1995) there is an agreement about the syllabus content for the European dimension throughout the country. The school subjects through which Europe is to be delivered are identified in the *Erlaß* as history, geography, social studies, modern languages and German, but beyond these specific subjects, European projects, visits and exchanges are seen to be important, as is the presence of foreign pupils within the classroom. Germany's geographical position in the centre of Europe gives rise to consideration of the countries of central and eastern Europe. All secondary schools have extensive and compulsory foreign language learning, with English dominating by a long way.

An examination of the syllabus documents of each of the *Länder* is beyond the scope of the research study. However there has been a most determined effort to integrate the European dimension into the programmes of study of all types of school over a long period. The Bavarian report in preparation for the 1990 *Erlaß* recognizes that subjects other than humanities have a role: 'Aber auch die übrigen Fächer, wie Religionslehre, Ethik, Deutsch oder die naturwissenschaftlichen Fächer, tragen zu den europabezogenen Bildungs- und Erziehungszielen bei.'[4]

This report also records that in the academic year 1989/90 seventeen in-service courses had been organized for teachers on Europe and lists many longstanding initiatives within the state to increase European awareness. In 1991/2 and 1992/3 the topic for special emphasis in schools was declared by the Minister for Education in Bavaria to be 'Europa entdecken – Einheit und Vielfalt'.[5]

The German pupils in our study did not consider themselves well informed about Europe in comparison with pupils in the other countries apart from Spain (55.2 per cent in comparison with the Netherlands at 79.2 per cent, France at 65 per cent, Italy at 64.3 per cent and England at 56.5 per cent). However, they were widely travelled, with only two pupils never having visited another European country. They gained a lot of information about Europe from their homes and from the media, but despite the large amount of curriculum time given to Europe (Green, 1995, has calculated 100 hours over the first five years of secondary education in social studies alone), they did not regard school as the main source of their knowledge. There could be speculation about the reasons for this and for their modesty about their knowledge. It could be that the awareness-raising is serving to make the young people over-emphasize their lack of knowledge: the more they know, the more they are aware of what they do not know. Certainly German young people have the reputation of being well informed politically and competent in foreign languages.

Interviews in one of our project's schools in Germany revealed that the pupils were learning a lot about Europe in geography, but when asked what else they would like to learn about Europe, one pupil complained that he would like to know more about politics than geography. He felt unable to make judgements because of his perceived lack of information. A teacher of English who considered that he had the skills to teach about Europe after thirty years of contact with the UK through exchanges and friendships, felt that the pupils take lessons about Europe for granted. He felt that they are too concerned about their own lives to think on a Europe-wide scale: 'I should like to see more openness amongst pupils to questions about Europe. They must have a dream if we are to make progress, but too many have the idea that "charity begins at home".' Does this comment reflect a changed attitude to the European Union in the experience of that teacher, from idealism to hard economic reality? Might it also reflect the strain of the enormous cost of reunification to the people of the former West Germany?

The German education system is able to provide both central planning and support for regional and local initiatives. It provides teachers and curriculum planners with outlines but how the topics are handled in class is left to the teachers themselves. The education system is held in high esteem by the population, and Germany is conscious of its position in central Europe, its close links with the countries of the eastern bloc and its status in the European Union as a co-founder member with France and as a leading force in economic development.

ITALY

In Italy there is currently no official body of knowledge on the European dimension which has to be taught in schools. Italian teachers are awaiting *la reforma*, a large-scale education act which will bring about massive changes to the whole system, including the curriculum. In view of this, few initiatives are currently being taken to include the EU in the teaching programme, although 1996, when Italy begins its term of office in the European presidency, will see the start of a research-based project, 'Discover Europe', in upper secondary schools. In the past, European-funded initiatives have been generally well received, and the schools which have participated have played a major role in the formation of a European identity amongst young people. A recent article in the *Times Educational Supplement* (19 January 1996) points to the very successful annual competition run by the state broadcasting service (RAI) which has now ceased, and the local financing of an education-for-Europe project in the Veneto region which operated in all primary and secondary schools alongside peace education, reported as now having 'gone off the boil'.

The teachers interviewed in the CRMLE study were all extremely pro-Europe and felt they ought to be teaching about it but were hampered by the constraints of the national curriculum as it stands. One teacher had taken the initiative and begun cross-curricular work on EU institutions. This had been very popular among the pupils but she had had to finance the work herself including photocopies of the material she had prepared. Yet both of the headteachers interviewed were very positive about Europe, saying that it was their duty to provide an awareness of Europe and to prepare their pupils for European citizenship. It would seem that decisions about the new Italian curriculum for schools will be crucial to the development of the European dimension.

At present Italy does not have education for citizenship, civics or politics on the syllabus as recognizable subjects. Europe is officially on the curriculum for 13 to 14-year-olds in history and geography though the history of the EU is not part of the programme. Most pupils learn two European languages except possibly those who at the age of 14 attend the prestigious *Liceo Classico* where they learn Greek and Latin. Italy has set up nine experimental schools, the *Liceo Europeo* where the European dimension features in the mission statement. In these schools it is compulsory to learn two foreign languages and to take part in visits organized to other countries. On a wider scale the *Istituto Tecnico e Commerciale*, a rough equivalent of the FE college in England, has an optional law course where European law plays a large part.

Italian pupils have been identified as very enthusiastic about Europe and among the keenest to learn. Their teachers are keen to include the European dimension in their work but are reliant generally on a lead from central government, which is slow to act. The reforms may include such large items as the raising of the school leaving age to 16, and the introduction of initial teacher training. It is to be hoped that the European dimension is not submerged in the upheaval which these two issues alone could bring about.

THE NETHERLANDS

Internationalism has long been considered important by the Dutch. This is due to the openness of their economy, their colonial past, their position as a major gateway in

Europe and the lack of any natural physical barriers on their borders with other countries. There has never been a question mark over the relevance of the European dimension in education since the formation of the EC.

The influential policy document *Widening Horizons* was published in response to the 1988 Declaration of the European Council of Ministers, and the 'European Platform' was established in 1990 by the Ministry of Education to co-ordinate European initiatives and projects for schools. This receives government support and funding to promote exchange activities and curriculum development. Teachers are encouraged to examine materials for their contribution to the European dimension, and a set of criteria are provided against which the materials may be judged. This includes reference to the kinds of issues which pupils are likely to encounter in their daily life in Europe, now and in the future, and to the discussion of positive and negative consequences of European integration for European businesses and individuals.

In the programme of reform in the Dutch education system and curriculum, the European dimension has not been a top priority issue. For pupils aged 10 to 11 in the Netherlands, Europe, including the EU, is a focus of their work in geography. In the secondary curriculum, it has at times been a compulsory element in the final examinations in history and geography. However, in an interview with one of our team, a Dutch teacher stated that she felt that the European dimension in schools is implicit rather than explicit. Another teacher no longer regarded the European dimension as a 'hot' item, and attributed its lack of explicit reference in the curriculum to the fact that it was no longer perceived as motivating for the pupils. Emphasis has been given in the Netherlands to education through Europe, to the encouragement of visits and exchanges, but since 1993 there has been an element of a European dimension in all of the subjects of the foundation curriculum for secondary education.

One teacher stated that the European dimension is present more in the environment than in the curriculum. For example a weekly television news programme called 'Jeugd Journaal' on Channel 3, is seen by all pupils at primary level, and teachers can then follow up any items of interest, according to the needs of the pupils and the relevance of the material. The programme has an international agenda, and it stands in marked contrast to 'Newsround', an equivalent broadcast in Britain, which has a more national slant on the news items covered. When asked where they received their knowledge about Europe, 44.1 per cent of the Dutch pupils questioned selected the media as their main source, whereas 56.8 per cent said their main source was school. The ambiguous response of the Dutch pupils in our study is probably due to this use of television in school. A further programme, entitled 'Klokhuis', is broadcast every evening at 1900 and is geared to older pupils. Fewer items are covered, but they are treated in greater depth and an attempt is made to understand what lies behind each issue. When European issues are dealt with, there is a less polarized presentation than might be the case in the UK.

The results of the analysis of the questionnaires from Dutch pupils indicates that they are the most aware of all the pupils in the survey of their European identity. They are also well informed about Europe, widely travelled and the most experienced in foreign language learning. This must surely derive more from the national context than from the school curriculum.

SPAIN

The introduction of the European dimension in the Spanish educational system coincides with the radical overhaul of the national curriculum instigated by the socialist government's sweeping educational reforms known as the LOGSE (*Ley Orgánica de Ordenación General del Sistema Educativo*). Spain joined the European Community in 1986, following a strongly pro-European referendum result. The attraction of joining was primarily economic and political. The immediate benefits to the country's economy are shown by the fact that in 1986–91 GDP growth was more than 4 per cent. Further, membership of the EC was seen as a means of consolidating the country's membership of the community of world democracies and as the final abandonment of its authoritarian and backward-looking past.

Rewriting the national curriculum provided an excellent opportunity for the government to formalize the country's commitment to Europe as an institution by inserting the European dimension into the education system. In fact, the preamble to the new curriculum states that the whole reform is set in the context of 'a common European horizon'. More specifically, the government responded to the European initiative by legislating on foreign language teaching, including references to Europe in the new programmes of studies, producing teaching materials on Europe, and by funding projects such as teacher and pupil exchanges, school links and the European dimension in teacher training.

In the case of foreign language learning at school, the new law requires that all pupils learn two foreign languages; the first is to be started at the age of 8, and the second at the age of 12. This replaced the previous provision of one language from the age of 11. The pupils continue learning these languages at least until the end of compulsory education at 16.

The European dimension appears in the content of the national curriculum, as a cross-curricular theme (*tema transversal*) along with health education, the environment, peace and equal opportunities. However, unlike the cross-curricular themes in the English National Curriculum, there are no specific aims, objectives or other guidance on teaching the themes. As in England and Wales, no provision is made on the timetable for these themes to be taught separately. If teachers wish to teach a certain theme as a separate subject they must create space in the timetable and devise their own schemes of work. One way in which some teachers have been able to cover the themes has been during the *ética* (ethics lessons). These are usually weekly lessons blocked against religious studies and which pupils can opt to study in place of religion.

The most tangible references to the European dimension are to be found in the programmes of study for the interlinking subjects of social sciences, geography and history, roughly corresponding to humanities in England. The general aim states that pupils should 'know, understand and critically evaluate their immediate surroundings, and the human and social community in its different spheres: local community, Autonomous Region, Spain, European Community and the international community'. There are ten topics which span the three subjects. Direct references to Europe can be found in the following topics:

- Environment and geographical understanding – the main natural features of Spain, Europe and the Planet;

- Population and urban space – demographic tendencies and problems in Spain, Europe and the less developed world;
- Human activity and geographic space – agrarian systems and spaces in Spain, Europe and the rest of the world;
- Political cooperation and conflict in the contemporary world – transformations and tensions in international relations, the process of European union, problems and prospects for peace.

Under the topic of 'the contemporary world', 11 to 13-year-old pupils are to study 'themes related to the political and administrative organisation of Spain, at local, regional and autonomous levels as well as the Spanish constitution and the institutions of the European Community'. The focus of the topics for 11 to 13-year-olds is explicitly at a national and European level and for the older pupils in a wider international context. Thus the most important years as far as the European dimension in the Spanish curriculum is concerned are 11 to 13. The objectives from the programmes of study are restated in the assessment criteria ('Criterios de evaluación por ciclos'): students should 'identify the main objectives and institutions of the EC ... and should use this knowledge to analyse the role of Spain in relation to the other member states through an issue which is relevant to current affairs'.

The integration of the European dimension within the Spanish national curriculum has benefited from the contemporaneous reform of the educational system as a whole. There is an emphasis on knowledge of the EU as an institution as well as some effort to tie this in with analyses of contemporary issues. The role of 'social science' as a discrete subject as well as the inclusion of politics or 'citizenship' within the humanities programme seem crucial. However, the outline of the programme is sketchy and provides minimal guidance to the teacher. Further, the Spanish pupils involved in our research did not consider themselves well informed about Europe and what they did know they felt did not come from school as the main source. Nevertheless, a large number of them considered themselves totally European (68.4 per cent) and wished to know more about Europe. One Spanish pupil stated as reasons for this: 'Because it is where we live and we're badly informed about it'.

It could be speculated that making pupils aware of European issues serves to increase their awareness of how much knowledge they lack, particularly since the Spanish pupils gave the media as by far the greatest source of their knowledge. Through the media the great issues for the European Union are discussed on an almost daily basis, though perhaps not in a manner that is immediately accessible to young people. In addition, the relatively few opportunities given to Spanish children to travel abroad on school visits may lead to a lack of confidence about knowledge of other countries in Europe.

ENGLAND AND WALES

The context in which the European dimension is presented in schools in England and Wales is the National Curriculum, which is fundamentally subject-based, with the three cross-curricular elements of dimensions, skills and themes. The European dimension does not feature as a dimension in its own right although that status is implied in the final report of the National Curriculum Modern Foreign Languages Working Group of

July 1990: 'Three important dimensions alluded to by the NCC are "equal opportunities", "multi-cultural perspectives" and what might be called "Britain in Europe and the world"' (National Curriculum Council, (NCC), 1990).

The European dimension is part of the theme 'education for citizenship' and is an aspect of international awareness (NCC, 1992). Pupils are required to develop knowledge and understanding of 'the variety of communities to which people belong: family, school, local, national, European and worldwide' (NCC, 1990). Two of the eight essential components for this theme contain references to the European Community. In *Education for Citizenship* (NCC, 1990), in 'Democracy in Action', the EC is cited alongside the United Nations Organization as a key organization in the twentieth century's attempts 'to promote international and global co-operation'. This is suggested as a possible area of study enabling pupils to 'participate fully as citizens'. In 'Work, employment and leisure' one suggestion for study is 'the roles of the UK government, EC, UNO and other international bodies in work, employment and national and international economies'. The aim is that there will be an increase in understanding of 'the social, political and economic contexts in which choices are made, and that the pupils will understand also the consequences of decisions for themselves and others'.

The role of the five themes of which education for citizenship is one, is to be related to all the National Curriculum subjects and religious education. They can be included in the prescribed content of the subjects or they can act as contexts for subject-specific skills. Their mere existence would seem somewhat surprising given the controversy which surrounded the work of the Whole Curriculum Committee, described by Duncan Graham in his book *A Lesson for Us All* (1993). Looking at the way in which the five themes permeate the whole curriculum, research was conducted by Gabrielle Rowe and Geoff Whitty as part of an ESRC research programme, 'Innovation and Change in Education: The Quality of Teaching and Learning'. Reporting in the *Times Educational Supplement* on 9 April 1993, they stated: 'Whatever curriculum audits showed, the themes had a rather shadowy presence in most of the schools we visited. It is difficult to see how they will recover from their present position when so much emphasis is placed upon the subject orders.'

In the paper reporting on the study (Whitty, Rowe and Aggleton, 1994) only a quarter of the schools surveyed had a written policy on education for citizenship, the least of all the cross-curricular themes, and the areas of the curriculum in which at least 50 per cent of the schools claimed to be including citizenship were seen to be personal and social education (PSE), English, history and religious education. Pupils in English schools in our survey were asked specifically in which subject they learnt about Europe, and geography and modern foreign languages occupied the central role with around 90 per cent of pupils recording that a lot, some or a little of their knowledge about Europe is gained during lessons in those subjects. History was next in importance with 68.5 per cent and then English with 58.5 per cent. Science, sport and maths offered fewer opportunities with scores of 35.2 per cent, 16.5 per cent and 13.6 per cent respectively, but nearly 60 per cent of the pupils in the survey felt that their knowledge came from other subjects not listed on the questionnaire, clearly a reference to PSE and tutorial programmes.

The 'slimming down' exercise of the National Curriculum led by Sir Ron Dearing, whose final report was published in December 1993, led to the cross-curricular themes being relegated to the back burner for a five-year period while the reformed Statutory

Orders for the core and foundation subjects were allowed to settle down. This is not to say that the Schools Curriculum and Assessment Authority is not continuing to examine aspects of the curriculum. Issues such as the environment, drugs and careers guidance may be brought into the limelight for a variety of reasons, and the current debate in the media about moral values and citizenship could well lead to a focus on these aspects at the end of the five-year period, but Europe remains a highly-charged political issue and it may be difficult for SCAA to give direction while the debate rages.

Currently, elements of the cross-curricular themes may well be established in personal and social education (PSE) courses in secondary schools and there may therefore be a European input in this area of the work of schools in England and Wales. The initial findings of the research group do not indicate that this is the case in many schools. In one UK school within the study personal, health and social education (PHSE) included two modules on Europe, developed by a teacher of languages and taught only by him. When interviewed about this he saw the European dimension modules as a way of underpinning the work of the modern foreign languages (MFL) department, to the extent that one of them had subsequently been incorporated into MFL teaching. He considered that the carousel model for the teaching of PHSE was less effective in terms of the development of relationships. The question then becomes one of the management of PSE programmes, and the confidence and willingness of non-MFL staff to embark on European issues.

An investigation into the content of some of the more recently published courses for PSE seems to indicate a minimum amount of attention to Europe. The PSE programme by Gurney (1991) has knowledge about Britain's membership of the European Community as one of its objectives for topic 37, 'National Government, Local Government and the European Community' in Pack 5, which is for use with Year 11. At the end of the pupil material on the system of government in the UK, there is a description in under 200 words of 'The UK in Europe'. This could be very useful material for the basis of discussion and it is a pity that the author has not included more ideas for exploiting it in the classroom or suggestions of where further resources on Europe are available. Europe was certainly a consideration for the authors of *Skills for Life*, published by Tacade (1994), but there are no specific references, though there are opportunities for teachers to extend the material according to their own wishes. Specific packages on Europe, such as *The European Election* (M.Kirby, 1994), *The Europe Kit* (M.Kirby, 1994), and *Europe ... What Everyone Needs to Know* (N.Edgar and A.Roe, 1994), provide a wealth of material but their acquisition by a school for PSE would depend on the willingness of the PSE co-ordinator to allocate sufficient time for their full use. Pat Gale and Jenny Hunt's 1993 manual for the integration of the European dimension into the structure and curriculum of colleges and schools, *Into Europe – Planning and Delivering the Curriculum in the 90s*, would require staff development time, ideally for whole school sessions.

A further factor in the promotion of the European dimension in the curriculum of secondary schools in England is the control exercised by OFSTED. The original OFSTED handbook includes reference to the cross-curricular themes in part 4 'Guidance: Inspection Schedule', and part 5 'Technical Papers'. In section 7.3(i) of part 4 'Quality and range of the curriculum: guidance', paragraph B 'Issues for consideration when reviewing evidence' there is an indication that the place of the European dimension in the school's curriculum could come under the scrutiny of the inspectors as they investigate the cross-curricular themes: 'In all schools, useful enquiries include:1. Is the curriculum planned to cover the requirements of the basic curriculum as set out in the Education Reform Act 1988 together with the cross-curricular themes?' (OFSTED, 1993). Part 5 of the handbook 'Technical Papers' deals with aspects of the inspection 'in which there is need for further guidance', and paper 2 makes further reference to cross-curricular themes under the heading 'Curriculum: general': 'Consider whole-curriculum planning for National Curriculum and non-National Curriculum subjects and cross-curricular issues, e.g. cross-curricular themes such as economic and industrial understanding, careers education and guidance, health education, environmental educa-tion and citizenship' (OFSTED, 1993).

The new OFSTED handbook, *Guidance on the Inspection of Secondary Schools*, on which inspections after April 1996 are based, is no more explicit on the European dimension than the original, though it includes 'an understanding of citizenship' in the considerations for the evaluation of the spiritual, moral, social and cultural development of the pupils. However, a key consideration is that the cross-curricular themes have always been non-statutory and remain so under the Dearing review. Schools need to satisfy inspectors in terms of the breadth and balance of the curriculum under both frameworks, but the inspection mechanism cannot be seen as a method of ensuring the implementation of a European dimension. However, where a school has extra-curricular activities involving, for example, travel to mainland Europe, inspectors may report on them in the section 'Pupils' Spiritual, Moral, Social and Cultural Development' as well as in the specific subject reports and in the remarks about the quality of education provided. Given the current significance of inspection reports in the development of schools in England and Wales, the opportunity for praise for such visits could be seen as encouraging.

In Scotland the European dimension enjoys a higher profile in inspections. It is not written formally into the inspection guidelines for secondary education but is inspected informally, and there is much encouragement for the European dimension to be part of the school's development plan. The Scottish Office Education Department has produced a report (1994) which outlines the priorities which are being pursued within the frame-work of the UK government's policy. The goal of the nine objectives is seen to be in line with the resolutions of the member states of the EC and the UK government in strengthening a sense of European identity in young people, while 'at the same time, preserving their sense of being Scottish and British' (p. 3). The Scottish Consultative Council on the Curriculum has produced a book to support curriculum development in this field, which contains practical suggestions about the integration of a European dimension into the work of primary and secondary schools. It is based on a publication from The Northern Ireland Curriculum Council which was the result of a project commissioned by the NICC in 1990. It contains suggestions for the integration of the European dimension in all areas of the curriculum including maths and science. In this respect Scotland and Northern Ireland can be seen to be ahead of England and Wales in their attempts to make the rhetoric of governments a reality in the secondary curricu-lum.

From the data collected by the research group, it would seem that questions about the place of the European dimension in the curriculum in English schools result almost always in a concentration of attention on history, geography and modern foreign languages. The 58.5 per cent of pupils quoted above for English (p. 45) includes 40.9

per cent who regard only a little of their knowledge of Europe as coming from that subject. The analysis of the European dimension in the National Curriculum by the DFE produced on a poster in 1991 indicates the role of these subjects as well as art, music and technology in secondary schools. This was part of a glossy pack produced to coincide with the British presidency of the European Union. The pack contained stickers and leaflets, but no real support for the integration of the European dimension into the curriculum. Maths and science were conspicuously absent from the poster.

Our research has shown that there has been little input about Europe in areas of the curriculum where Europe has not been explicitly included in the statutory orders. The importance of the national requirements in England has to be underlined, not least because they are relatively new phenomena in English schools. An additional and highly significant factor is that of the curriculum overload caused by the programmes of study in the National Curriculum in England which was all too evident in the interviews with teachers. This along with the many other innovations of the 1988 Education Reform Act has meant that initiatives outside that which is statutory have had a low priority and that the core and foundation subjects have been the main focus of attention.

The original Programmes of Study for history were among the most controversial of the National Curriculum, partly because of the stipulation that in school twentieth-century history ends twenty years ago. The Statutory Orders of 1991 indicate for Key Stage 4 that 'Pupils should be taught to understand how the world in which they live has been shaped by the developments in twentieth century history ... but it is not a course in current affairs' (DFE, 1991c). It goes on to state that 'pupils should have opportunities to prepare themselves for citizenship, work and leisure' (DFE, 1991c).

If citizenship includes the exercising of one's right to vote in European elections, then the history curriculum cannot have a role in this aspect, because the exclusion of events in the 1970s and 1980s in Europe means that the membership of the UK since January 1973 of the EEC is not part of the statutory programme of study. The Dearing review (SCAA, 1994) made history optional after the third year of secondary education and the most recent history to be taught remains the legacy of the Second World War. A comparison of the work of two history teachers, the one in England who is now beginning to teach about the Cold War in Y9, and the other as a geography and history teacher in France embarking on an explanation of Maastricht in the equivalent of Y10 and complaining about the lack of suitable material, highlights one difference in emphasis in those two member states. It would seem a lot to expect of most secondary school pupils in England to make a connection between the Cold War and the politics of the EU in the 1990s, let alone to understand the spirit of cooperation and mutual support in the Europe of the 1990s from a background of Europe torn apart by war and bloodshed, hostility and tension.

The role of geography lessons in learning about Europe is seen by many pupils as central, yet the National Curriculum by no means offers the study of European countries the pride of place which the French curriculum offers to its pupils in the equivalent of Y9. In one of the schools in the survey Y10 pupils were interviewed about the tasks they had been set about Europe and they identified labelling countries on a map in Y8. The geography teacher recalled that task as virtually all they had done on Europe, and could not understand why the pupils otherwise associated geography with Europe. His department worked on a topic basis and he felt that there are better examples of the topics in other countries. However, the association of 'other countries' with geography seems clearly established, and for many of the pupils interviewed, Europe was just that. If one lesson experienced two years previously could remain so firmly in the mind of the pupil in the interview, how effective a whole series of lessons on Europe could be in the development of the skills and understanding necessary for citizenship of Europe.

The Dearing review of the statutory orders for geography, which, as with history, makes the subject optional after the age of 14, would seem to give emphasis to Europe in that the thematic work with pupils from 7 to 11 and 11 to 14 requires a range of geographical contexts which includes the European Union. However the study of places in Key Stage 3 does not make a European country compulsory. As geography is 'one of the most heavily restructured of all the national curriculum subjects' (Maxwell, 1994), it is difficult to assess whether Europe has gained in significance through Dearing or not. Much depends on the extent to which geography teachers use the context of the EU, and that in turn depends on the increase of material about Europe in course books.

Modern foreign languages departments are generally well placed to promote the European dimension through the choice of authentic materials and contexts. Only with the introduction of the National Curriculum did it become compulsory for pupils in secondary schools in England and Wales to study one foreign language throughout the five years. On the one hand that was regarded as a major achievement especially in the light of the lack of suitably qualified teachers, but on the other hand the crowded pre-Dearing curriculum in the primary school meant that there was less opportunity to include languages at the primary stage. Where foreign language teaching is now being offered, and there are indications that it is growing in strength, it is nearly always, for historic reasons, French. The report *The TES/CILT Survey of Modern Languages in Secondary Schools* (CILT,1996) indicates that this has been the largest factor over the past five years for secondary schools' returning to offering only French as a first foreign language in year 7. Despite the many initiatives to develop the teaching of other languages and the range of possibilities offered in the National Curriculum, England's foreign language teaching continues to be greatly dominated by French, with German, Spanish and Italian following. That in itself restricts the extent to which teachers of modern foreign languages can offer pupils a broad insight into mainland Europe.

The Dearing review has further meant that from the age of 14, pupils are able to choose to do a short course in their foreign language, amounting to half of the curriculum time originally envisaged. The CILT research (1996) indicates that one in four of the 1140 schools in the survey is planning to offer the short course and that 80 per cent of those schools predict that there will be fewer pupils taking a full course to examination level. A stark contrast emerges with other countries of the EU where foreign language learning enjoys a much firmer position in the secondary education of young people.

'Developing cultural awareness' has remained part of the Programmes of Study for Modern Foreign Languages in the Dearing proposals (SCAA, 1995c), and the ability of pupils to communicate in the foreign language goes hand in hand with a growing understanding of the people in the countries where that language is spoken. In the BBC programme 'Teaching Today', Mary Ryan examined more closely the concept of 'cultural awareness' and stated: 'It's more than simply learning about French cafés or German shops. It's also a gradual understanding and developing understanding of the people, their customs, their attitudes etc.' (BBC, 1994).

The programme showed how contact with native speakers in the form of foreign language assistants promotes cultural awareness. It is through their work in MFL that pupils can encounter and communicate with people who speak another European language and begin to develop their own European identity. The Areas of Experience also give a valuable context for the promotion of the European dimension, in particular Areas C 'The World Around Us' and F 'The International World'. Parallels for the examination of current issues in the pre-16 curriculum for MFL can be found in other countries of the EU. However, not all schools have a foreign language assistant on the staff, and where the assistant is shared for economic reasons with another school, it may not be possible for many classes to have contact. The introduction in 1996/7 of an EU-funded programme, whereby intending teachers from EU member states work as teaching assistants in UK schools, will help to disseminate information about other countries, as well as support the European dimension. In order to widen the experience of secondary school pupils, it has been decided that French, German and Spanish assistants are unlikely to be placed in secondary schools. Imaginative initiatives such as this are an important way forward.

Modern foreign language departments in secondary schools may well have a more international agenda than that of a European dimension if they encompass languages beyond those of the EU such as the languages of great world powers, for example Russian and Japanese, and as those of ethnic minority groups such as Urdu, Bengali and Panjabi. In addition the multicultural aspects of the teaching of European languages has been taken seriously in the inclusion in text books of material from non-European countries where the target languages are spoken. However, one teacher in a multicultural inner-city school in the research study expressed a regret that those children learning a community language as their NC language in Y7 were not learning a great deal about Europe beyond the UK, and hoped that they would be allowed to begin to learn a European language at a later stage. In that school too, there was a desire to undertake an exchange visit with France, but also a recognized need to find a school with a similar multicultural ethos in order to encourage wide participation. As a similar situation was discovered in France, happily contacts have now been facilitated, but the schools could have sought the advice of the Central Bureau, which supports and makes possible a range of international visits and exchanges.

This same teacher of modern foreign languages in a multicultural school was concerned also about the political message of the European dimension, as she was conscious of a lack of enthusiasm for Europe in certain sections of society. Her colleagues in the humanities department were aware also of the more global perspective. The headteacher's comments showed a personal commitment to Europe but a sensitivity to the nature of his school:

> If you are asking me do I feel it would be positive for people to bring the European dimension into their teaching in a cross-curricular way, I think that is true, but not if we become totally euro-centric because particularly in the nature of this school which is a multicultural school we have to be careful not to just concentrate purely on Europe but have a much broader view than that.

This view was echoed by some of the student teachers in our study (see Chapter 5).

The headteacher of a Roman Catholic school in a small town in England did not feel that there would be resistance to explicit references to a European dimension in the school's documentation although they did not currently exist, despite the high level of interest and involvement in Europe in many areas of the school's activities. He saw his school as 'a part of the tradition of European Christendom', but maintained that 'European' should not be 'stressed at the expense of any outside-Europe ecumenical emphasis'. When asked about his concern for global issues, he felt that Europe would be a starting point and that 'a strong united Europe would be a beacon to the rest of the world'. It is significant that both headteachers, though euro-enthusiasts, placed Europe firmly in a wider context, albeit for different reasons.

Many teachers in schools in England talked of increased workloads caused by the National Curriculum and other innovations, and that was a factor in deciding the priority which could be given to Europe in their schools. There was almost no evidence of any in-service training in this area, courses being confined largely to the implementation of the curriculum and assessment requirements of the core and foundation subjects. Teachers also saw the work overload as having an influence on the frequency of organized visits abroad for the pupils, and in one case the need to prepare for OFSTED had to take priority. There was also an awareness of new regulations for taking pupils on visits and of the huge responsibility which such trips involve, valuable though the experience is for the pupils.

Above and beyond the context of the National Curriculum, there would appear to be in England a great deal of support for teaching about Europe. The research indicates a number of cross-curricular initiatives, including visits abroad, and a desire on the part of enthusiastic europhiles teaching subjects other than those most closely associated with Europe to include a European dimension in their work. There is much work around the theme of Europe being tackled in primary schools. The work of the Central Bureau is well known in most schools. A recent package of information sent to schools from the Central Bureau gives details of the Socrates project and invites subscriptions to Eurodesk Schools' Service. One of the leaflets has the question 'Is your school making the most of Europe?' on the front cover. If the schools can afford the annual fee (£50.00 + VAT for secondary schools) then they will receive up-to-date information about how to attract European funding, incentive enough in times of cut-backs in budgets to look to the European dimension.

The Central Bureau has 100,000 ECUs available from Brussels for promoting multinational partnerships between schools in 1996–97. It is likely that there will be 160–70 co-ordinating schools and 360–400 participating UK schools in that year. Of course, the figure remains small when compared with the total of approximately 5000 state schools in the country. Nevertheless, over a few years the number of schools involved in transnational projects is not insignificant. Research needs to be carried out in order to evaluate the extent to which pupils' perceptions and attitudes towards Europe are affected by involvement in partnership programmes and to see whether a sense of European identity and citizenship is heightened as a result of such an involvement.

The DFE's policy document of 1992 in response to the 1988 Resolution laid considerable emphasis on the role of Local Education Authorities (LEAs) to initiate and support the European dimension. Many have been able to fulfil this role by appointing key personnel and by allocating funding to projects. What schools have not been able to do on their own has often been co-ordinated by the LEA throughout a county or borough. An example of this is an exchange programme in a metropolitan borough where schools on their own cannot raise enough participants to make an exchange viable, or in a county where exchanges with schools in Germany or Spain attract the second foreign language learners who are often relatively small in number.

Among the most prominent LEAs in promoting the European dimension is Humberside, which has produced its own European Awareness policy statement. In his foreword to the 1994 document, the Director of Education, Michael Garnett, writes of the young people in his schools and colleges as 'part of the first generation of new Europeans' and stresses their need to be well informed about Europe. Rising above the arguments about federalism and monetary union, he points to events in the recent history of Europe which have brought an end to tension and suffering, and given new opportunities for economic growth. His words hark back to the origins of the European movement in the post-war period, and are in line with the attitudes of many of the young people in our study. The document includes suggestions about the integration of the European dimension into the National Curriculum subjects, and discusses issues of resourcing, funding, staff development and evaluation. Fundamental to the work on the curriculum is the high priority given to European Awareness which refuses to be constrained by national policy: 'It needs to be clear in our curricular thinking that European Awareness is seen to be of equal status to other cross-curricular themes and this message is reinforced by its inclusion in The School Curriculum in Humberside' (Humberside County Council, 1994).

Humberside is not alone among LEAs in its work on the European dimension, but there are also many LEAs which are unable to give it anything like such a priority. Many questions arise. How far does the priority given to the European dimension depend on the enthusiasm of influential people? Is there a lack of resources? Has the diminishing role of the LEA in areas where many schools have 'opted out' meant that the LEA has had to claw back on its activities, thereby marginalizing initiatives beyond those which are statutory? To what extent does the impetus for the European dimension stem from the activities of local industries and commerce? These and many other questions remain beyond the scope of the research study. LEA work on the European dimension is patchy, but where it exists it is well supported and publicized by the Central Bureau.

From a national perspective, a sharper focus for the work cannot now be envisaged until the five-year settling down period following the Dearing curriculum review is over, but the new space created by the slimming down exercise allows schools to develop their own programmes, and education for citizenship is beginning to re-emerge as an educational priority. It may well be that by then the shortcomings of the 'Anglo-American' nature of the National Curriculum referred to by Morrell (1996) will be apparent to politicians. From the data which the research team has collected it would seem that English pupils are less well informed about Europe than most of their counterparts in the other European countries, but that they wish to know more. The UK could be a main focus for European exchanges as so many young people in other countries are learning English, but wider contacts can only be initiated by more diversification in language learning in England and by a sensitive incorporation of education about, through and for Europe into more areas of the curriculum.

NOTES

1.   'I was anxious to ensure the training of the citizens of tomorrow.'; 'It's about building a France which is strong, united and bound together by its values and its culture, an open and

welcoming France, capable of conversing with different peoples and of cooperating with other nations.'

2. 'Resolution on a policy for Europe'.
3. 'The goal of education must be to awaken in young people the consciousness of a European identity.'
4. 'However, the remaining subjects such as religious studies, ethics, German or the sciences also contribute to the cultural and educational objectives which relate to Europe.'
5. 'Discover Europe – unity and diversity'.

Chapter 4

The Educational Politics of European Citizenship

We have observed in previous chapters that, despite the political rhetoric (partly generated by the May 1988 Resolution), a tangible and coherent implementation of the European dimension by many of the Union's member states has been limited. The inclusion of the education clause in the Treaty of Maastricht has done little to accelerate curriculum change at the national level. Indeed, it could be argued that, while the Treaty gave the European dimension legitimacy, it undermined the 1988 Resolution through its reaffirmation of subsidiarity. As a consequence, in a number of the countries in our study, young people consider themselves ill-served by a conservative and cautious curriculum and by a media unable to *mediate* the complexity of the issues. Apart from a few pockets of activity, evidence of learning about Europe at any level of sophistication is scarce.

In this chapter we will draw upon a further component of the CRMLE study, the governors' questionnaire administered to schools in England and Wales. This sought to illuminate key issues related to the implementation of the European dimension. These are: what is the relationship of European citizenship to the general notion of a European dimension in the curriculum; to what extent is the introduction of European citizenship seen as political education; to what extent might European citizenship form part of an entitlement curriculum for European youngsters? In order to do this we need to attempt to reveal some of the values attached to citizenship by educators and decision-makers and to re-examine the place of political education in the curriculum.

We have seen that one way of looking at Europe in an educational context is via the distinction and progression: *about Europe*; *through Europe*; *for Europe*. This distinction is not an easy one to conceptualize in curriculum planning terms. In the school governors' questionnaire, therefore, respondents[1] were asked a general question first, namely, if they felt the European dimension was a worthwhile addition to the curriculum. The governors' data, given the small size of the sample, needs to be treated more qualitatively than quantitatively. Nevertheless we can be confident that the general response to the inclusion of a European dimension was a positive one. Philosophically, the European dimension was seen to represent an essential part of the curriculum. The benefits of its inclusion were mutual both to the students and to the future of the EU as a constantly changing socio-political entity. Many expressed the view that it was only by changing the views of our young people that progress towards greater tolerance and understanding would be made. Moreover, it was their right to have access to the knowledge and understanding of Europe: 'It is a necessary means by which to educate young people to the European ideals. This is not functioning through the media.'; 'an essential element: students have a right to access their own heritage'; 'vital at the present time: the union was and has become inevitable and necessary'.

The few negative reactions to the question were confined entirely to the practicalities involved in finding space for it on an already crowded curriculum or to the problems of integrating it into the curriculum: 'yes, but cross curricular delivery is never very successful' and 'it shouldn't be an addition, rather part of the whole'.

Given that there appears to be near consensus on the value of the European dimension among those in charge of implementing the school curriculum, can it be that it is only lack of curriculum time which inhibits its inclusion? Is it possible, on the other hand, that it is a lack of clear definition of what the European dimension might be and lack of directives from central government about its value which are creating the conditions for procrastination? We can explore this further through the project data. Respondents were asked what the European dimension should actually be about. Should it be about an awareness of the employment opportunities offered by European integration, about an awareness of the social and political issues resulting from that integration or about European citizenship? Clearly these categories are not mutually exclusive and respondents were offered the opportunity to accept all three. Table 4.1 demonstrates quite emphatically that awareness of opportunities and an understanding of the issues are key elements of the European dimension for school governors. European citizenship, while not being advocated by quite as many respondents, nevertheless appears a perfectly acceptable component of the European dimension for a majority of governors.

Table 4.1   *The European dimension should be about ...*
(N=44)

	Yes	No	No response
Awareness of opportunities	42	1	1
Awareness of European issues	43	1	
European citizenship	37	4	3

The evidence from the data so far suggests that 'contested concepts' (Carr, 1991, p. 374) might indeed have an uncontested common core. Most teachers of subjects such as history, mathematics and modern foreign languages (MFL) could easily arrive at a consensus of basic principles about the nature of their subject. They might disagree strongly about the methodology or approach to the teaching of their subject (chronological as opposed to thematic teaching in history, content versus process in mathematics, the amount of explicit grammatical knowledge needed in MFL), but the common core binds them together. From the pupils' data we would have expected the European dimension to have no such substantive core of consensus. Why, therefore, is there a mismatch between the beliefs of those in charge of the curriculum and the descriptions of those that receive it? In order to give a tentative answer we need to dig deeper. Does that common core remain uncontested when it comes to the practical application of principles in a classroom setting or when cross-referenced with notions of identity and political convergence? As we shall see, the concept of citizenship itself is far from unproblematic. Yet the presentation of citizenship in *Curriculum Guidance 8* for the National Curriculum of England and Wales (NCC 1990) is entirely non-conflictive. In this document the European Community is merely portrayed as 'an attempt to promote international and global co-operation' (p. 5) and pupils are to 'investigate links Britain has with communities elsewhere in the world' (p. 26). This serves to anaesthetize any ideological conflicts that might exist between communities and organizations. The rest of the data collected from school governors in England will hopefully illuminate some of the internal debates going on within respondents and help us understand better the precise nature of the European dimension. First let us look briefly at the changing idealization of citizenship.

CHALLENGES TO TRADITIONAL NOTIONS OF CITIZENSHIP

National citizens within the EU find themselves in the perhaps unique position of being asked simultaneously to *take on* and *create* the concept of European citizenship. While it is possible to talk about people who are citizens of Europe rather than just inhabitants of Europe (Lodge, 1993), it can be argued that these people merely posses the *badges* of citizenship not the substance of it. Heater (1992, p. 53) describes these badges as: the right to vote, the right to hold a passport and an emblematic focus of one's loyalty such as a flag. EU citizens have all these. Since 1995 we have, in addition, the prospect of a common currency, the Euro. What is manifestly lacking however is a sense of loyalty to one's fellow (European) citizens and the obligations that pertain thereto. Thus citizens of Europe we *are* and *are becoming*. As we have argued earlier, the European Union is adolescent. This is the first challenge to the traditional and (formerly) stable notion of citizenship.

The second challenge comes from social and ethnic mobility both intercontinental and, more substantially, intracontinental. Ethnic groups from outside Europe (or outside the EU) have, since the second world war, brought into being multi-ethnic and multicultural states which continually question former identities based on historical cohesions. It has been estimated that by the year 2000, one-third of the population under the age of 35 in urban Europe will have an immigrant background (Broeder, 1996). Changing work patterns, the transportation of goods and the establishment of European multinational companies are contributing to an unprecedented mobility and transient workforce within the EU. When an infrastructure to facilitate this mobility is added to the equation, the EU is confronted with the possibility of an increasingly displaced population over the next ten years.

The third challenge is to the role of the nation state as the sole provider for its citizens. The power of the nation state has a direct bearing on the individual citizen's inability to see himself/herself operating outside the nation's citizenship boundaries. Arguments against world citizenship, as Heater (1990, p. 229) points out, link citizenship directly to the tangible reality of the nation state. Only if the state fails in its contract to the people (protection and welfare in return for loyalty and duties) might they begin to look beyond the state, to seek a higher political relationship (p. 230). The problem with this view is that it depicts the traditional notion of citizens as a cohesive whole. Nevertheless, it might be fruitful to consider how nation states might fail in their contract with their citizens. Social exclusion and the inability to deal with poverty might be seen by many as examples of the state's breaking of an unwritten contract. Yet these exclusions have always existed. Is it the case that the increasing presence of a supranational state offers a more desirable alternative? There is some evidence of this in our pupil data from Germany and Italy but it is neither clear cut nor conclusive (see below, p. 62). In Britain the promotion of individualism, the attack on the welfare state and the erosion of local democracy (Carr, 1991, p. 373) may be perceived as a nation's inability to provide the very social cohesion which gives it its raison d'être. The 1980s produced a 'politically acceptable' underclass of citizens – the long-term unemployed and disadvantaged ethnic groups (Dahrendorf, 1994, p. 15). These groups eventually may have come to the realization that they were unable to access the economic fruits of the market economy. The locus of authority may thus have become displaced and it may be a natural consequence that problems of law and order increased as a result of the exclusion of this underclass. In the UK the focal point of loyalty, in recent years, has also been displaced. Regional polarization through economic divergence and the promotion of individualism have undermined traditional symbols of allegiance. The British government has declared that it has no 'selfish, strategic or economic interest in Northern Ireland' (Downing Street Declaration, December 1993) and the British monarchy and the union of Scotland with England have, of late, been severely undermined.

The fourth challenge is that of cultural transmission. While the tabloid media may seek to give an impression of a nation's cultural sovereignty, the quality media and, more importantly, the electronic media are able to make the citizen aware of cultural similarities across national boundaries which are more closely influenced by social status and income than by national identity. It is possible therefore that a middle-class professional Briton may have closer cultural affinities with his/her French counterpart than with a working-class Briton. Breakfast routines, television viewing habits and attitudes to education are only a small selection of indicators of this trend. Perhaps even more pertinent in our discussion of young people is the recent example of the Tottenham Hotspur football fans who reported (BBC News) no diminution in their loyalty to the club no matter how many foreign players that club might field on a Saturday afternoon.

The fifth challenge is that of the gradual encroachment of individualized social, moral and cultural values over traditional class, religious or ethnic solidarity. While there is no empirical evidence (Halman and Ester, 1994) that the penetration of individualism is consistent across all domains, nevertheless even a fragmented impact on traditional values will have a repercussion on the way geographical groupings perceive the notions of citizenship.

It is within the context of these challenges to the overall notion of citizenship that the debate on what the European dimension should contain needs to be conducted. Moreover, the question needs to be asked as to whether teachers feel confident to teach the European dimension given the responsibility it carries with it in the face of these cultural and constitutional challenges. One responsibility is contending with the perception that some educators and parents may have of the European dimension as a form of political education.

THE EUROPEAN DIMENSION AND POLITICAL EDUCATION

Of the six countries in the project, only Germany and the Netherlands had an explicit political element in their curricula. Obstacles to the introduction of political education have traditionally (in the UK at least) been associated with the maturity of the learner, the problem of bias and the relative importance of politics to the rest of the curriculum (Heater and Crick, 1977, p. 21). As these authors point out, none of these objections stand up to scrutiny. In the case of the first, politics is the art of choosing wisely among alternative courses of activity. Choice is determined by attitudes and attitudes are formed fairly early in a child's life. There is no strength, therefore, in the argument that school children are too immature to handle political and social issues. In the case of the second, it is true that some teachers may themselves be anxious about political indoctrination. Others may fear that pupils, parents, headteachers or governors might think them biased or incapable of presenting an argument in a balanced way. Yet, as we shall see from the project data, there is little or no evidence to suggest that teachers are suspected of applying personal bias when teaching controversial subjects (and none in any studies we are aware of). In any case, the question needs to be asked as to whether European citizenship can be deemed to be a controversial subject. Its status is not contestable. Its implications for the citizen are complex and may be seen as controversial only when juxtaposed with an exploration of national citizenship. The third objection has been partly answered above. Failure to prepare pupils for citizenship and reluctance to help pupils see arguments with more than just personal referents is a failure of education. It is natural for individuals to differ about interests and ideals (Heater and Crick, 1977). For young people not to understand and celebrate diversity may have catastrophic consequences for our increasingly complex and multi-layered societies. Yet in UK schools anything resembling political education is limited to self-exploration and tolerance of others in personal and social education courses which are additions to the mainstream curriculum and held in low esteem by pupils.

In the study, school governors were asked to comment on whether they thought European citizenship might lead to political indoctrination. Three themes emerged from this data. The first is that citizenship, by definition, cannot be controversial. It is a condition which, once conferred, cannot be ignored or denied. Some respondents linked citizenship to a discussion of political issues. Here too it was felt that there was an inbuilt safeguard against indoctrination in that the shades of political opinion and the full array of EC parties would offer a sufficient range within which to present the possibility of making informed choice. We could add to this argument that the perception of ideology as a binding force for political action has decreased. A manifestation of this is the emergence of single-issue politics over class-based struggle as the political motivating force for many young Europeans. As Rayou (1994, p. 33) points out, while politics appears to have little appeal to pupils in secondary schools, it was young people who carried out the major campaigns against racism, poverty and famine in the 1980s. Instead of reshaping society, Rayou continues, young people today seem to prefer creating networks of micro-solidarity. The second theme to emerge from the governors' data is that it could indeed lead to indoctrination but that the teacher could be trusted to steer a course through the controversial minefield: 'it might be if the subject is not carefully presented'; 'teaching should be honest and factual – just like in citizenship and social issues'; 'only if the teacher is excessively politically motivated (might it lead to indoctrination)'. Only one respondent saw a real danger of indoctrination in that European citizenship was 'becoming an increasingly emotive area' and that it was difficult to believe that it could be taught in a neutral way. The final theme to emerge was that its controversiality was its *actual* power. British pupils were politically naive and undereducated. This made them vulnerable to indoctrination and extremism and teaching was a defence against this. Pupils, according to these respondents, had 'inbred (hostile) attitudes' which needed challenging. As one respondent said: 'this may be the opposite of indoctrination'.

Yet, as Carr (1991, p. 374) also points out, in a general citizenship context, without an effort to clarify the complex relationship between citizenship, democracy and education, education for citizenship will become an empty slogan. We are aware that in the UK pupils are shielded from politics, state institutions and the international community (Bell, 1995, p. 32). We have also observed that this protection is likely to be more harmful than beneficial. How might a teacher, therefore, tackle controversial issues, themes which at the European level divide political parties as well as nations? Heater (1990) suggests a model for citizenship education based on knowledge, attitudes and skills. Under *knowledge* he proposes that a teacher should be able to provide pupils with facts, an understanding of what those facts imply or entail and an understanding of the personal role that the pupil has in relation to that body of knowledge. It would be useful to add here an understanding of the role of identifiable groups within the pupil's immediate frame of reference: family, friendship groups and so on. Under *attitudes* Heater proposes that it is the teacher's duty to provide self-understanding, respect for others and respect for values. Under *skills* he proposes: intellect and judgement, communication and action. As we can easily detect from this model, citizenship education is certainly not value-free. The moment knowledge-based objectives are linked to attitudinal objectives, competing values result. Respect for others necessitates more than a mere tolerance of the cultural values of others. Teachers may be able to adopt a responsible approach but not an impartial one. Impartiality in the field of European citizenship education implies that there can be no challenging of existing values, that systems and constitutions can only be asserted and confirmed, not modified and restructured. Thus, when EU policy conflicts with the policy of the national government of a member state, we have to ask whether the very exposure of the conflict by a teacher suggests a failure to maintain impartiality. An example of this is the controversy on political advertising (*Guardian*, 27 December 1995, p. 1: 'Political EU Ads Spell Trouble for Major'). Here the EU's (presumably democratic) decision to launch, through the Commission, a campaign promoting the Euro, is seen by Eurosceptics in the House of Commons as 'pushing the rules beyond the threshold of what is acceptable'.

Perhaps there is no clearer example of value-laden education for citizenship as in an examination of the apparently conflicting principles with which the EU itself now functions. We shall now examine this notion and relate it to a possible European dimension in the curriculum.

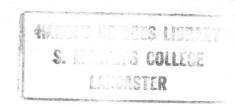

THE EU AS A VEHICLE FOR INSTRUMENTAL GOALS

The Common Market was originally created for economic purposes. Its overarching principle was the free exchange of goods with the intention of bringing about the increased economic prosperity of the member states and to increase the economic potential of those states to operate both on European and world markets. Even now, the EU's agenda appears to be an economic and financial one based on international capital acquired and processed through European multinationals (Sultana, 1995, p. 9). The student's personal role in this might be to consider vocational qualifications in order to access the wealth that the EU is able to generate more effectively. Indeed European agencies are actively promoting vocationally linked pupil mobility. Trade, after all, is based on competition between groups and between nations. Studies among language learners have demonstrated a clear tendency towards learning a language as an instrument for accessing wealth (Macaro, 1997; Chambers, 1994). As we have seen, Bordas and Giles Jones (1993, p. 93) report that young people's perceptions of Europe as a community, that is, as a group of people who live together and cooperate with one another, is not very widespread. As we write (December 1995) the media portrays an EU locked in an economic struggle between stronger countries able to converge towards monetary union and weaker countries unable to do so by the deadline of 1999. We have *fast track* and *slow track* countries, central countries and peripheral countries, with economics exerting simultaneously centripetal and centrifugal forces on the latter. Economic imperatives have become paramount. Individual liberty and rights are expressed in terms of the freedom to create wealth through entrepreneurial endeavour.

Also as we write, television presents us with startlingly different images: that of young Britons, on a stage, joyfully welcoming in the target language the competitors in the European football championships to be held in the summer of 1996 in England. To be noted for the benefit of our discussion elsewhere on identity and ethnicity, in this television presentation, we see the inclusion of young people from ethnic minorities acting as these 'ambassadors'. We would not wish to belie the undoubted benefits accruing to cross-cultural exchange and to language learning from the positive images in this programme. Nevertheless the ironic reminder that big profits underpin the whole structure and purpose of these football championships is a difficult one to shake from one's mind.

Running in parallel to the market forces, the Social Chapter of the Treaty of Maastricht reflects a different view of the concept of the democratic superstate and, by the implication of subsidiarity, the nation state. This counterweight to the commercial nature of the EU is not an invention of the 1990s. The origins of the EU's social policy can be traced back to the European Coal and Steel Community where special provision was made for the retraining of miners who had been made redundant, thus correcting the distortions resulting from the Common Market (Moxon-Browne, 1993, p. 152). This social policy gradually came to impinge on many more areas of EC's activity such that it now infiltrates the domain of domestic politics and challenges party political dogma (ibid.). The rejection of the Social Chapter by Britain in 1989 and the subsequent negotiation of the opt out clause, is therefore none other than a rejection of a vital strand in the socio-political development of the EU. The impact of this rejection on education can be identified, for example, in the exclusion of the official Lingua programme from British secondary schools.

Social policy is the element of the EU's programme aimed at providing social cohesion. In this model of democracy, therefore, there is an intrinsic interest in promoting shared values about human rights, dignity and in the celebration of cultural diversity. As Bell reminds us (1995, p. 23), education for European citizenship is about these positive principles. They are, after all, internationally recognized principles. Nations and governments, such as the UK, who sign up only to the instrumental functions of the EU, can only be promoting a one-sided view of the democratic role of the state, a market model with individual liberty as its single and core principle (Carr, 1991). Yet some would argue that the status of citizenship is removed from the vagaries of the market. Citizenship is a non-economic concept (Dahrendorf, 1994, p. 13). A person's rights as a citizen are not dependent on the contribution that he or she makes to the economy. Moreover, as Halman and Ester (1994) report, a number of authors see a theoretical distinction between *utilitarian* and *expressive* individualism where the former emphasizes personal interests and material success, the latter giving prominence to individual autonomy, creativity and the uniqueness of the individual. Individualism does not have to be synonymous with a lack of altruistic values and a denial of the importance of the community. Thus, not only can European economic policy be balanced with European social policy but the simplistic distinctions between the functions of the Union are being progressively obscured.

Any exploration of the above tensions in European citizenship education must include an exploration of these values. Nevertheless, lack of EU policy on citizenship has contributed to the dominance of instrumental ends rather than cultural process and change. Given the challenges made to national identity and traditional notions of citizenship the time is propitious for a European dimension in education to incorporate a balance of instrumental and social functions of Europe. Those on the political right would argue that this dual track European dimension is tantamount to political indoctrination. We have attempted to show in the above discussion that it is not.

DUAL AND MULTIPLE IDENTITIES

It is important when considering the nature of citizenship to observe that it is not synonymous with notions of identity. National citizenship, for example, is not directly tied to national identity. Scottish people identify with their specific cultural symbols while operating within the citizenship boundaries of the UK. Moreover, examples such as that of Switzerland suggest that there is no evidence that citizens have to share the same language or the same ethnic and cultural origins. Nevertheless, our layers of identity are increasing. As Habermas (1994, p. 31) notes, we are living in a functionally ever more differentiated society where an ever greater number of persons acquire an ever larger number of rights of access to and participation in an ever greater number of subsystems. For each individual the number of memberships in organizations multiplies and the range of options expands. One of the functions of citizenship is therefore to provide an environment where an individual, faced with these layers of identity, can operate without conflict or stress. We have already observed (in Chapter 2) that English pupils have a much weaker association with the concept of European identity than their mainland equivalents.

Table 4.2   *Percentage of respondents by country to the question 'Do you think of your-self as European?'*

	Not at all %	Only partly %	Yes, totally %
England	39.8	41.6	18.6
France	17.4	41	41.6
Germany	10.5	26.3	62.6
Italy	4.3	41	54.7
Netherlands	2.6	7	90.4
Spain	6.4	25.1	68.4

But does an identification with supranational symbols and constructs bring with it a dilution of national identities? A comparison of Table 4.2 and Table 4.3 suggests that this is not the case.

Table 4.3   *Percentage of respondents by country to the question 'Do you think of your-self as [own nationality]?'*

	Not at all %	Only partly %	Yes, totally %
England	4	25.7	70.3
France	6.7	16.2	77.1
Germany	18.7	32.7	48.5
Italy	1.4	13.7	84.9
Netherlands	0	6	94
Spain	1.8	5.3	93

The comparison between the tables is worth exploring in detail. Dutch youngsters, while scoring the highest in terms of European identity also scored highest in terms of identifying with their own country. Spanish and Italian youngsters, similarly, appeared to have little or no psychological difficulty with dual identities even though the actual scores are less pronounced. What is particularly interesting about these three countries is the very low scores for *not at all* 'own country'. If we take Italy as an example, one might have imagined that the current national political situation (corruption trials, and calls for regional separatism by the Northern League) might have led Italian youngsters to perceive a supranational power as offering a solution to national chaos. The pupil interview data demonstrates that this is only partly true and the answer is more subtle. Italy, according to the interviewees, is not presented (by, for example, the media) as a central player to the Brussels project. In addition, the southern regions of Italy (from which half of the Italian sample came) are presented as the confines of the European periphery. Thus youngsters reported perceiving themselves not only on the margins of national political-economic activity but also on the margins of European political-economic activity (Adelman and Macaro, 1995, p. 42). An assertion of identity with both levels was therefore an attempt to sustain layers of identity other than a mere regional one. This reaction is particularly illustrated in their response to the media's presentation of European issues:

Interviewer: How do you feel when you hear about it [Europe] in the media?

Pupil 1: *Well, for example yesterday I heard that they'd joined up three more states and that we'll talk about fifteen not twelve states. I felt a lot better because you feel some changes are coming about and that they're always trying to go forward ... we musn't stop, we've got to keep going.*

Interviewer: Do you feel proud or bored?

Pupil 1: *Bored? No not at all ... very happy and proud.*

Pupil 2: *I get a bit annoyed because we're a bit isolated from this European community. Perhaps other countries like England judge us badly.*

Pupil 3: *It depends, when I hear about Bosnia it's depressing ... in terms of the community. I'm always happy if we're all united without any distinctions ... and then each one has their own culture ... but we're all part of the same continent.*

The so called 'central countries' of the EU have a greater number of differing responses (Tables 4.2 and 4.3). Germany, while scoring high on European identity, scored the lowest on national identity. Clearly historical events and contemporary issues related to unification may well have led to a confusion of notions and concepts. Habermas points to a democratic deficit brought about by the process of German unification which has been 'effected more at an administrative and economic level than by enlisting the participation of its citizens' (Habermas, 1994, p. 21). In the case of France with its slightly lower scores for European identity, there is a firm reassertion of national identity. English pupils in particular seem to experience discomfort with dual identity. In other words young people from the less 'prominent' countries of the community are able to show allegiance to a new and developing Europe but hold it essential to maintain an equal allegiance to their national identities.

What might be the cause of the inability among English pupils to accept dual identities? Is it the case, as Bell (1995, pp. 5–15) would argue that dual identities for some nations are difficult? That national sentiments, history, heritage and mythology coupled with the nationalism which is fostered by competition in trade consolidate national identity to the exclusion of all others? Certainly this would seem to have some influence. Yet we have argued above, in the challenges to static notions of citizenship, that the UK is, in cultural terms, no more a homogeneous country than other European states. Indeed the slightly lower scoring than expected in terms of British identity may reflect the number of non-white respondents in the English sample of the pupil survey (see Chapter 2). The CRMLE study in general places the media as the strongest influence on pupil attitudes. Given that large sections of the English media continue to represent Europe as an arena for economic and political conflict, it is not difficult to infer that this is one of the main causes of young people's attitudes to dual identity. By the influence of the media we do not confine ourselves to the 'Up Yours Delors!' and 'Frog Off Our Lotto' little-Englander mentality of the tabloid press.[2] A perusal of all spectrums of the English press during a week in December 1995 (Madrid Conference) gives the reader an overwhelming impression of discord and conflict. Ministers squabble over the name of a future European currency. The Prime Minister's language is peppered with references which have echoes of 'us and them', and 'fighting Britain's corner' while in the same breath talking about 'our European partners'. Clearly the positive advances of the last fifty years: unprecedented peace within the Union, economic progress, greater tolerance of cultural diversity and the upholding of human rights through a European court, is subordinated to newsworthy disagreements. If we compare this with a cross section of the French and Italian media for the same week, we are presented with far fewer images of conflict. Moreover, Morrell (1996, p. 19) draws our attention to the statistic that English youngsters watch an average of eighteen hours of TV per week and that their viewing diet is almost entirely Anglo-American.

Single identity is thus perpetuated by a lack of debate about local, national and supra-national levels of solutions. Are schools in a position to rectify this imbalance? Should schools in England explore and encourage the advantages of a dual identity? Here the governors' responses begin themselves to differ. About a third of respondents felt that this was not the school's role or that it was important to retain as the stronger element an identification with the country of citizenship: 'emphasis should continue to be a British identity with an awareness of European involvement'. A second group saw no weakening of national identity through the promotion of dual identity: 'Our English and British culture remains important but there is room for both this and European identity.'

This group also saw its functional value in solving problems whereby dual identity promoted greater cultural and racial understanding and awareness. Indeed one respondent put it more prophetically:

> as the UK plc runs out of steam, it would make sense to think of ourselves as English/Europeans in a Europe of the regions. It has potential advantages in dealing with the Irish problem – we might get rid of a lot of psychological junk from the past.

A small group of respondents raised an even more subtle issue. These were governors who reported that they were in multicultural schools. For them their immediate efforts were aimed at local integration. They were already in the business of creating a secure and positive environment where dual identities could thrive. Thus while these respondents pointed out that a further level had to be managed carefully, they did express the opinion that the European element could only enhance their present strategy. Further research on cultural identities may indeed reveal to what extent diluting strongly adhered to identities through the addition of a supranational ideal might help take the sting out of racial conflict at the local level. However if national politicians are not able to set an example even at the cost of relinquishing some of their own power in this way, it is unlikely that this desired end will come about.

There is a further but related theme which emerges from the governors' data and in fact from the research data in general. This is connected to perceptions of Europe as an affluent coterie of nations remorselessly acquiring wealth at the expense of the Third World. Within this perspective, the question of European identity takes on a very different aspect. For the ethnic minorities of the union, adherence to the European ideal entails a dilution of their original identities, which might have been strengthened by empathizing with third world countries. In terms of multicultural development, educators are placed in a dilemma: on the one hand they might opt to promote multiple identities and the European ideal, thereby decoupling the image of ethnic minorities from the concept of Third World poverty. In so doing they would run the risk of returning to a racial assimilationism of the type described by Fanon (1952). Alternatively they could minimize the impact of European identity in multicultural localities in order to give saliency and confer positive status on the culture of origin of the ethnic minority group. In so doing they might run the risk of polarized racial and cultural positions. This latter view is, to some extent, the one taken by Sultana (1995) who argues that the presence of multi-ethnic groups in Europe means that it is important to critique the promotion of the European dimension in schools and that learning 'for' Europe carries an implication of learning 'against' others. Claiming that teachers involved in the European dimension are 'acting as technicians for agendas set by Brussels', he argues for a systematic insertion of opportunities in the curriculum to discuss questions relating to ethical, political and social choices regarding European integration. It is at this point where the overlap between citizenship and identity becomes problematic. Heater (1992, p. 62), quite rightly in our view, proposes that European citizenship must be understood in the limited sense of the EU. For him citizenship is a 'legal-political status in its strict sense and consequently can be exercised only in the context of a polity'. Identity on the other hand, unfettered by constraints of government, constitution or civil organization, is free to go beyond citizenship towards its natural cultural home. A related situation is that of former East Germans living in one culture but identifying with another – a phenomenon known as *innere Emigration*. The question of multiple identities is clearly a complex one. No wonder one school governor commented: 'given the multiracial nature of our school this (a third identity) presents an interesting challenge!'.

What is gratifying is that the pupils' interviews in the CRMLE study show unambiguously that they have considered the question of Europe in the world and that they are aware of Europe's responsibilities. There is no evidence that, in their excitement about progressive integration, there is a neglect of the global dimension. It must be recognized, however, that identities are in a process of transition and that the rate of transition may increase as a result of new citizenship boundaries being created by European integration and, indeed, global mobility. Thus what Byram (1992) calls *self-ascription* of identity, the passing from one group allegiance to another, will become a feature of ethnicity in our schools. There is some evidence that teachers are not always sensitive to the delicate nature of these transitions.[3]

POLITICS AND IDENTITY IN THE NATIONAL CURRICULUM

We have examined in previous chapters the response to the European ministers' 1988 resolution. This response was to be implemented in different national contexts. The first type of context is the one found in those countries with a (at face value) prescriptive national curriculum but which, in reality, allows high levels of freedom and interpretation at the school level (e.g. France, Italy). The second is with an authoritarian curriculum, backed by a strong inspectorate, which designates cross-curricular themes and dimensions but does not specify parameters for its evaluation. Such an educational context is that of England and Wales. In this section we will look at three subjects in the National Curriculum for England and Wales and try to understand to what extent curriculum planners have made educational choices which might reflect a political ideology and how those choices inhibit the possibility of a cross-curricular implementation of the European dimension.

(i) History

History in the National Curriculum ends just at the point when Britain became a member of the European community. Although the history document recommends that pupils should learn 'how far and why European countries drew together between 1945 and 1970', this is in Key Stage 4 and history is not compulsory beyond Key Stage 3. By virtue of the very fact that Britain's joining of the community is not an 'historical fact' it promotes an 'us and them' perception of Europe. The historical divisiveness of Europe is not counterbalanced by the more contemporary convergence and peace. The Historical Association's own view (quoted in Morrell, 1996, p. 13) is that: 'unless there is a clear rationale and commitment by history teachers to providing pupils with a balance of British, European and world history ... Key Stage 3 will be heavily and disproportionately Anglocentric and over-political'. There may therefore be a tension for history teachers wanting to make a positive contribution towards European citizenship and their mission to deliver the National Curriculum. We have explored the fear of political indoctrination at some length. This is perhaps nowhere more an issue than in the realm of history teaching. It was coincidentally a history teacher interviewee who, on the subject of controversiality in the European dimension, expressed it thus: 'I think that in any issues which are controversial ... if you give a personal view, I don't see a problem as long as it is obvious that it is a personal view.' When it comes to the subject of History itself, however, there is some evidence to suggest that history teachers stress the importance of responsibilities over rights and that they may, by over-emphasizing a notion of professionalism, misunderstand that their subject is unavoidably political (Davies, 1995). Should pupils be allowed to question whether European history is merely an arena for incessant nationalist, imperialist and ideological struggles? Is there, in fact, a hidden curriculum in History, a set of political pressures to emphasize conflict rather than accord? If a hidden curriculum exists, it is possible that it is being nourished by the inherent tension in the European educational debate, between notions of unity across Europe and those of diversity according to the needs and traditions of individual states (Bell, 1995, p. 146). Curriculum planners have their own agendas. Any decision about curriculum content and emphasis is not made in an ideological vacuum. While this is an unavoidable reality, the ideology behind curriculum planning has, at the very least, to be made explicit and transparent, focusing and explaining how curriculum selection addresses the needs of pupils, communities and states. In this way history educators would be able to question what the individual needs of those states actually are.

(ii) Modern Foreign Languages

If a re-evaluation is required in the teaching of history between the needs of the learner and the obligations demanded by the state, it is also essential in the field of modern languages. Hagen (1992) has admirably exposed the mismatch between language provision via the National Curriculum in England and Wales and the needs of the increasingly internationalized and Europeanized commercial environment. The notion that the purpose of foreign language learning was in order to go out there and bat for British industry is now not only outmoded but possibly harmful. European industry is increasingly multinational in character. British schoolchildren have the distinct prospect in the future of working either for a foreign employer in the UK or for a British employer in another European country. This has two fundamental consequences. First, an educational policy based on concentrating for five years on a single language does not provide the linguistic base upon which to build future language learning. In a rapidly changing commercial environment, competence in two foreign languages and the first language are now a minimum requirement for European managerial and secretarial posts. As Macaro (1996) argues, at least part of foreign language provision in UK schools should be concerned with 'emancipating the language learner from the classroom', providing the learner with the language learning autonomy to pursue the learning of the same or different languages in future and unknown contexts. Second, in the new financial Europe, going out and winning contracts will not be the primary function of managers (Hagen, 1992). Rather, a company's future will depend on the ability of individuals to work as part of an increasingly international team. For this they will need multilingual collaborative skills in which code-switching is common place. All these factors have a direct consequence on the methodology that teachers employ and demonstrate a need for greater diversification of foreign language provision. Interestingly, France's national curriculum places foreign language learning squarely in the context of educating for European citizenship. France's central government judges itself to have a crucial and interventionist role in promoting not only the uptake of language learning but also the diversification of language provision within the wider European context (Legendre, 1995).

There is a further factor which must be addressed. We have suggested earlier that language learners in England see the purposes of language learning overwhelmingly in instrumental terms: being able to get by in Europe while on holiday and in order to improve their opportunities of obtaining eventual employment. While there is nothing objectionable about these purposes, it could be argued that they need to be interlocked with an intrinsic motivation for language learning – learning a language in order to get to know better the people whose native language that is. The evidence quoted earlier suggest that this purpose is not valued by young learners in England. By contrast a recent Swedish survey of 15,451 European graduates from thirteen Western European countries (Lenning, 1995) found that respondents, when judging the quality of a place of work, were looking for an openness to foreign cultures, a good social ambience and good communication with other local and international colleagues. Can it be that the more limited perspective of English 13-year-olds is merely due to lack of maturity or is it something inherent in the foreign language curriculum which perhaps does little to transcend cultural barriers and fails to provide an environment for multiple identities? As Byram (1992) has pointed out, the phenomena which mark the boundaries between groups are as important as the phenomena which appear to be the core of the group's identity. Language as a boundary marker needs to be counterbalanced by language as a means of accessing an understanding of 'the other's' culture and institutions. For future workers to operate efficiently as members of multinational teams, they will need to make that transition towards accepting and integrating foreign cultures into their own reference framework. At the present time we have no evidence that language learning is achieving those ends. There is, indeed, evidence that the teaching of the target culture is characterized by a huge variety of content and style (Byram, Esarte-Sarries and Taylor, 1991). It is moreover so characterized by a one-way flow of information from teacher to learners that we need to question whether current methodological trends at best postpone and at worst inhibit in-depth understanding and celebration of target cultures.

(iii) English (First Language Teaching)

In the domain of first language teaching also, the National Curriculum has sought to preserve the notion of a single identity and a single culture. First, the prescriptive choice of literature, largely limited to a classical canon of texts aimed at promoting the English language as the 'essential ingredient of the Englishness of England' (former Education Secretary Kenneth Baker quoted in Byram, 1992) and little chance of comparative literature studies, has once again marginalized the possibility of a cross-cultural curriculum. The underlying suggestion is that the essential role of important literature is to help define national identity rather than deal in universal truths. Second, the emphasis on Standard English, taken to the extreme of suppressing materials on language diversity and change,[4] is in essence a strong message to an ethnically diverse society that their identities need to be assimilated. Lastly, as Hagen (1992) again points out, the notion of English as an international language needs to be qualified. What is by and large spoken internationally is 'broken English'. As a consequence, an awareness of language and how speakers employ communication strategies could become a positive contribution in the first language curriculum to inter-cultural awareness in a European context.

Underlying this theoretical critique of the National Curriculum are objectives which set out to provide an equilibrium by looking at Europe as a social as well as an economic living space (Bell, 1995, p. 121) and demonstrate that there are indeed similarities between the European dimension in education and aspects of multicultural education.

THE EUROPEAN DIMENSION IN THE CURRICULUM AS PROCESS

It is becoming evident from the lack of clarity and definition about what the European dimension in education actually is, that what European educators will be dealing with here in the coming years is a process rather than a body of knowledge. National support in the form of documentation is too vague and uncommitted and in-service training all too rare for a coherent and standardized programme of study to emerge. Furthermore, we have to bear in mind that not all teachers will express a commitment or a confidence to undertake teaching of the European dimension. Finally, the EU itself is unlikely to provide the momentum to bring about change. This is ironic if we take a working definition of subsidiarity as meaning the most suitable level (local, regional, national, state or European) at which to take decisions. Given that the European dimension was agreed by a council of ministers, and given its current ineffectiveness at the state level, it would seem logical to look for implementation at the European level where this is not happening at the regional level (see Chapter 3).

For this dimension to the curriculum to take root, however, there would seem to be a need to identify, at the very least, some possible bases for development. We wish to propose two such bases. The first is one which finds its pedigree in political education, the other in comparative social anthropology. The two are not mutually exclusive but they do demonstrate a clear divergence of emphasis according to teaching capacity and need.

1. Political education basis

If we established a process programme of European dimension in the curriculum based on traditions of political education, we would have to expect a number of procedural outcomes. By this we mean that the whole school curriculum and/or individual subjects' schemes of work would outline a progression from teaching pupils about Europe, through Europe and for Europe. This would contribute to and run alongside a parallel development of awareness leading to interaction which in turn would lead to empowerment through an understanding of citizenship. It would be essential that this citizenship contain a reference to the possibility of *action* at a number of levels. A third development would involve moving from an instrumental perception of the value of the European Union to a balanced perspective incorporating both instrumental and integrative functions of membership to the Union. These three developments are illustrated in Figure 4.1.

Figure 4.1 *Political education*

about ⇒ through ⇒ for Europe
awareness ⇒ interaction ⇒ empowerment
instrumental ⇔ integrative motivation and values

Taking pupils beyond mere awareness could be considered as part of their entitlement curriculum. As individuals and groups they would be accessing the opportunities which European integration offers. However, young people need also to be taken beyond the socialization process brought about by decision-making at levels far removed from their immediate sphere of influence. Let us take a concrete example of a learning project.

Pupils could take part in a simulation of a conflict situation such as the following. Residents are informed of the proposal of a district council to build a road through a nearby green area or park. The residents are opposed and think they have a good case at the local level, based on observation of traffic flows and information about the effects of increased pollution. How might an effective protest campaign be mounted? Clearly applying pressure at a number of key levels might represent the best chance of the road not being built. Knowledge and understanding of potential action can: (i) enable the citizen through collaborative action to exert pressure at the local level by lobbying council representatives and trying to persuade council engineers of alternative solutions; (ii) enable the citizen through collaborative action to exert pressure on their local member of parliament, enlist the support of national environmental agencies and cite governmental policies; (iii) enable the citizen through collaborative action to enlist the support of European agencies, cite European policies on environmental issues and enlist the support of their MEP, ultimately to have recourse to a European court. They might also make contact with relevant protest groups in other European countries. In other words, pupils could be helped to understand their rights as citizens at a number of political levels.

It is the knowledge and potential to take action which moves the individual beyond passive socialization to empowerment. The above example, as a model of pupil learning for future citizenship, is unlikely to be delivered transversally – right across the curriculum. One solution would be to define the European dimension as a separate subject as in Germany (*Sozialkunde*) as teachers would feel more competent to teach it.

However, this would be to deny the process value of the understanding of citizenship, confining knowledge to a narrow band of teachers. An alternative is via PSE programmes. A final alternative is via a number of 'lead' subjects: geography, history, science, modern languages, with other subjects offering a more limited contribution.

2. Comparative social anthropology basis

This theoretical model enables pupils to study the culture and institutions of each member state or groups of member states analysing them into categories of knowledge and action essential for the informed citizen. Taking, as an example, some of the issues from the CRMLE study questionnaire: traffic regulations, regulations on residence and qualifications to work – these could be compared and contrasted structurally. The rights of the lay person and the powers of law enforcement could be examined first at the document or law level, which may differ, second for their homologous function in the different cultures. Halman and Ester (1994) report substantial cross-cultural variation in individualism between Western countries. This could be explored. Using this method of investigation could provide the beginnings of a content for a comparative curriculum which makes explicit those elements in each culture which are unique as compared to the majority which, though superficially different, serve the same or similar functions. As an alternative model this offers a number of advantages. First it takes commonalities as its starting point, then identifies differences as either elements particular to the needs of a given culture or as possible 'good points' which might be emulated by all. The role of the family and the care of the elderly are typical of topics which would fit this category. Second, it is likely that pupils' imaginations will be fired more by having people rather than Europe's political institutions as a starting point for an understanding of Europe. Third, it allows solutions to social issues to be examined at local, regional, national, state or European levels. Health education, pollution and equal opportunities could be examined according to the matrix proposed in Figure 4.2. Lastly, this model would seem more amenable to a full integration across the curriculum.

Figure 4.2   *A comparative social anthropology model*

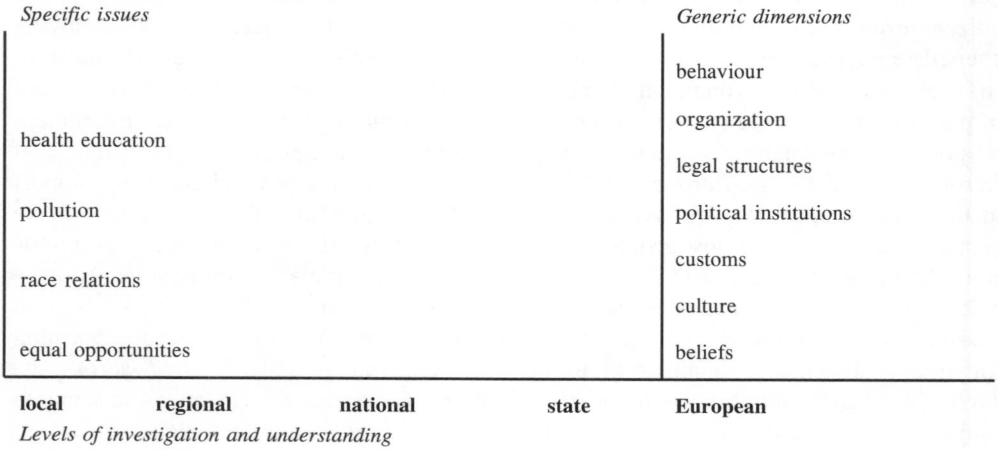

Specific issues	*Generic dimensions*
	behaviour
	organization
health education	
	legal structures
pollution	political institutions
	customs
race relations	
	culture
equal opportunities	beliefs

local	**regional**	**national**	**state**	**European**

Levels of investigation and understanding

Table 4.4   *Approaches to the European dimension in education*

1	2	3	4	5
Actively promoting citizenship	Examining the institutions for their effectiveness	Historical perspective of the EU 1950–92	School trips for language learning	Historical and geographical knowledge of Europe
Active involvement in principles of democracy and social justice	Making judgements about speed of unification	Understanding the workings of the EU institutions	Language learning for jobs, business and tourism purposes	
Understanding of rights and obligations	Discussing pros and cons of federalism	Keeping abreast of European Union developments		
Debating political issues within a *European Union* context	A European dimension in history, geography, MFL and English	School trips to other European countries for cultural awareness and cultural comparisons		
Involvement in intra-European school projects	Extended language learning, e.g. geography taught in French	Language learning in a cultural context		
Examining the media for bias		A European dimension in history, geography and languages		
Analysing various levels of decision-making to see where decisions are best made				
A European dimension in every school subject and/or specific course in PSE programme				

These two bases on which to proceed need far greater examination and elaboration than this book allows but we offer them for discussion and possible research and development. Moreover, they are compatible and can dovetail within the same process curriculum. This is represented in Table 4.4. Here schools move from approach five to approach one as the process of awareness and understanding increases and as the tensions inherent in a multi-layered model of identity and allegiance begin to be resolved within the staff themselves and through working with the pupils. That this process of exploration and understanding is not currently going on has been alluded to in previous chapters. That the time is ripe for the process to begin is, however, evident from the CRMLE study. Governors of schools in England were asked to identify which of the five ápproaches outlined in Table 4.4 they felt were acceptable in their school. They were free to declare as many as they wanted as acceptable. This was in order to get a feel for how far they were prepared to advance towards the kinds of aspirations projected by the 1988 resolution. Table 4.5 gives a summary of the responses.

Table 4.5   *Number of respondents who thought approaches in Table 4.4 acceptable*

Approach 1	30
Approach 2	19
Approach 3	36
Approach 4	36
Approach 5	35
Total	156

These results surprised us. The picture painted by the survey data was that most schools in England were rarely above approach 4. In only a few of the examples cited in Chapter 3 were schools giving the (albeit neutral) perspective of EU institutions (approach 3) and there were no examples of schools examining EU institutions for their effectiveness or making judgements about speed of unification. It was therefore an encouraging sign that these 'guardians of the school curriculum' should see approach 1 (the one researchers envisaged as being the most controversial) as acceptable.[5] Clearly Table 4.4 invited respondents to demonstrate general orientations not specific curriculum selection, and indeed some qualified their responses. Interestingly it was trigger words such as 'federalism' which led governors to refrain from ticking the approach 2 box. One governor commented on approach 1: 'I am dubious about actively promoting citizenship ... the line between active promotion and indoctrination is a narrow one.'

This comment suggests that a clear understanding of the meaning of citizenship has not yet been arrived at in schools. On whether pupils should be involved in examining issues at all levels (as suggested in the matrix above) governors were almost unanimously in favour. However the following is a selection of interesting comments:

> Local yes, national yes, but at a European level, only for comparison against a Denmark or a Greece for example, not at a federal Europe level, because each country has different standards and expectations.

And by contrast:

> Yes (all three levels). Any education should seek to encourage pupils to look outside their immediate sphere of activity, so that they can place that *immediate* sphere in the wider context and question constructively its partial or total validity.

> Yes, ideally this should be the case. Are the staff able to do this? I doubt it in some cases. We are working against strong cultural forces.

Finally, one respondent made the pertinent observation: 'But do we do it for local and national levels now?'

As a final question, governors were asked whether they would be happy with a European dimension input which stressed the convergence of European cultures. Whereas dual identities were generally seen as promoting an environment of tolerance and understanding, converging cultures posed a greater problem for respondents although the responses were not as hostile as we had anticipated. Those who were against, implied a denial of the existence of a common European culture, 'a forced superstate with a phoney culture', instead stressing the richness and strength of diversity. Others did not feel it was the school's role to 'bring European cultures closer together'.

A majority of respondents were unquestionably in favour, as summarized by: 'be positive – convergence of cultures'. Those in the middle, while appearing reasonably happy with cultural convergence, pointed out that it was not diametrically opposed to retaining diversity:

> Taking the USA as a model, it has national 'identity' but many local sub-cultures (e.g. states). It is unlikely that the strength of European national (state) cultures will ever be substantially eliminated.

As we have intimated earlier, it may be that the search for a definition of the European dimension in education may serve teachers and learners better in the form of a process of discovery rather than as a product which can be packaged, a fixed syllabus with a defined lesson content, ready to be taught on a given day. It is in the dialectic of the process that the planning, the implementation and the monitoring of the European dimension will see its most effective re-evaluation. In a sense, the questionnaire administered to governors mirrors that process of discovery, analysing reactions to concepts such as citizenship, identity and political indoctrination.

It is clear that the development of the European Union in recent years has been overshadowed by arguments over sovereignty and federalism. This, in part, has led to an inertia in the curriculum with regard to the European dimension. A process approach sees the very fact that it is currently a controversial governmental issue as the kick-start to its greater visibility in schools.

NOTES

1. Unless wanting to make a specific point, we have not in the analysis of this data made a distinction between headteachers, teacher governors, parent governors, etc.
2. Headlines which appeared in the *Sun* newspaper, 1 November 1990 and 6 January 1996 respectively.
3. In a project involving Japanese children in English schools, researchers report significant instances of teachers advising parents to speak English at home (Fletcher and Yamada-Yamamoto, 1994).
4. The 'Languages in the National Curriculum' materials commissioned by the National Curriculum Council, then suppressed.
5. Of course, not all respondents ticked the boxes for approaches 4 and 5 but ticked 3 and 1, thereby suggesting that the acceptability of 4 and 5 was implied. In other words, 4 and 5 are incorporated in the 'higher levels of commitment' to the European dimension.

Chapter 5

UK Student Teacher Perspectives

A powerful message to emerge from the research data is that young people living in the EU today would like to know more about the Europe that they inhabit and would like to have the tools at their disposal to help them interpret the stream of data that comes their way via the media and their own personal experiences.

The responses from the pupils in Chapter 2 stressed their desire for more knowledge. The documentation referred to in Chapter 3 highlighted the need for high-quality teaching material in order to promote the European dimension in the classroom. The evidence from the various curricula also showed clearly the wide disparity in the amount of information that different pupils were receiving in different countries. The political issues dealt with in Chapter 4 underlined how contentious an issue the European dimension can become if national curricula are juxtaposed with the needs of a developing European perspective.

Standing between the pupil and this body of knowledge and array of processes is often the lone teacher. All educators are forced to define a broad area of knowledge on which to focus their teaching programmes. The criteria behind this selection need to be transparent and justifiable. The teacher can be the facilitator of processes allowing pupils to debate, argue, explore and wrestle with some of the thorny issues associated with the difficult subject of the European dimension. What are the qualities regarded as desirable in such a teacher and how are they to be trained? We might begin to arrive at a definition of these qualities by first examining the input of initial teacher training.

As all of the CRMLE group were involved in initial teacher training in England at the time of the original research it seemed appropriate to consider what role, if any, the European dimension should play in the training of future teachers. If the pupils interviewed reported that they wished that their schools would act as information mediators and help them to decode the media input about Europe and evaluate all the impressions they were receiving from travel and family, then it seems pertinent to ask whether their future teachers are being trained to help them to do so.

Student teachers do not fall from the tree. They arrive on their training courses with as much intellectual, emotional and psychological baggage as any other cohort of similar professionals. They have many preconceptions about what teaching is all about, mainly from their own personal experience of receiving teaching from school through to university or college. They remember their own teachers and how they themselves learned, and bring with them experiences of the world of work or of parenthood. These preconceptions are deeply ingrained and take a considerable amount of effort to bring to the surface and to examine critically. If we want our student teachers to be able to reflect upon past experience and evaluate it critically, then we must give them the tools to do this effectively and the space in which to accomplish it. Does the model of initial teacher training in England and Wales provide these tools and space?

Wubbels (1992, p. 137) has persuasively argued that student teachers' preconceptions are thoroughly embedded and that 'teacher education programs fail to influence student teachers' conceptions that they bring to the teacher education program'. Because all student teachers bring with them ideas about teaching and what should be taught in varying degrees of conceptual development, it can take a considerable amount of time and ingenuity to probe all the different beliefs and values. Wubbels again (p. 140):

> Student teachers often think that the real job of the teacher is to explain things clearly and for years and years they have experienced this when they were students themselves. Teacher educators, however, want them often to realize that the primary aim of education is that students learn and understand.

When it comes to something as diffuse and controversial as the European dimension, student teachers may react in predictable fashion. They may reject the whole notion as either too 'progressive' or 'irrelevant' and bound up with the theoretical model of the higher education institution and therefore not grounded in the reality of everyday classrooms or else of no particular concern to them because it does not relate squarely to their subject, issues of class management, better methodology or assessment.

Whereas student teachers' main concern is acquiring 'coping strategies', the fast-changing European context will need practitioners who can match their personal development to a much broader and shifting educational context. Schön (1987) has characterized such teachers as 'reflective practitioners'. Such people are able to examine critically their own subject knowledge and pre-training experience as well as their performance in schools as classroom practitioners. They can reflect upon what has preceded their training and are able to differentiate (taking into account general theory and localized factors) that which was useful from that which was less helpful. They can also evaluate their own feelings of competence in delivery of their subject, can fine tune their management and methodology and are open to advice. Eventually they will be able to reformulate their personal theories of teaching and learning. Although there may be some debate about the precise definition of what it is to be a 'reflective practitioner', nevertheless it aptly portrays teachers who are willing and able to take on board opinions and views which may be new and challenging – and by definition *unsettling* – and mould them to their own purposes.

As we have seen in preceding chapters, the European dimension is difficult to define precisely in terms of subject content and schemes of work. However, if teachers of the future are going to confront their pupils with the realities of living and working in a European context and if they are going to help their pupils interpret the daily diet of news from and about Europe, then they are going to need to have their own preconceptions about the subject and the teaching of that subject challenged during their initial training.

   The European Parliament and the Council of the European Union are under no illusions about the significant role that teachers have to play in disseminating information and understanding about the European dimension. Following Articles 126 and 127 of the Maastricht Treaty, they launched two extensive Community action programmes, called SOCRATES and LEONARDO which comprised both the educational and vocational measures outlined in the Maastricht Treaty. Almost every aspect of SOCRATES is designed to promote the European dimension in higher education, in schools and in teacher education programmes: 'The principal objective of SOCRATES is to give as many young people as possible the chance to add a European dimension to their studies and preparation for working life' (European Commission, 1993).

   This is justified in paragraph 4 of the explanatory statement issued upon the establishment of SOCRATES: 'Education and training have new roles to play in the process of economic and social change which Europe now faces. This will mean deep-seated changes in the education and training systems of the member States' (European Commission, 1993).

   The rationale is further developed in paragraph 8: '*(This mission) is to shape open, critical and creative spirits* and direct them towards initiative, practical application and communication. It should strengthen the spirit of citizenship in a democratic and caring society based on Europe's cultural heritage' (Our emphasis).

   There is little room for ambiguity here. The language is direct and uncompromising. Many transnational projects have been set up in order to promote the European dimension in the training of teachers and their trainers and the ARION initiative in particular has concentrated principally on the development of networks of those involved in teacher education. Action 1 of the LINGUA programme is specifically designed to promote language skills in the community by helping modern languages teachers either to upgrade their existing linguistic skills or else to take on new languages to teach. Action 3 of the newly designated COMENIUS programme for schools deals specifically with in-service training for teachers in the field of the European dimension.

   Of course initiatives alone will make no difference if there are few people to take advantage of them. It is reasonable to assume that those interested in these European initiatives may already have some commitment to the ideals enunciated in paragraphs 4 and 8 quoted above. Challenging the preconceptions and stereotypes of those student teachers undergoing initial training can be an uphill task.

   We now turn to look at how that task was undertaken at one of the universities included in the CRMLE research project.

ITE EUROPEAN AWARENESS CASE STUDY

Having examined, in the main part of the CRMLE study, the views of school pupils in some depth, and having explored through interviews the opinions of teachers and headteachers, the team of researchers decided to elicit from a cohort of trainee teachers their views on European awareness. This was felt to be appropriate since trainee teachers represent the future teaching force and will be carriers of innovation into schools. If the 'top-down' policy initiatives from community and governmental quarters do not seem to have made a widespread or substantial impact, as we have seen in Chapter 3, do we need to look to the next generation of teachers to integrate a European dimension into the curriculum with more conviction? If newly-qualified teachers have had an opportunity to consider European awareness issues during their training, and also to share ideas for integrating European themes into curricular and cross-curricular areas, might a 'bottom-up' approach be more successful than the 'top-down' one referred to earlier?

THE QUESTIONNAIRE

In an attempt to answer these questions, a case study was carried out in one of the higher education institutions taking part in the research and involved student teachers at the end of the secondary Postgraduate Certificate in Education (PGCE) course. A questionnaire was distributed to the whole cohort of students (286) in July 1994, and 130 (45.5 per cent) responses were received from across all the subject disciplines represented (science, mathematics, modern languages, English, geography, history and classics). The aims of the questionnaire (Appendix A2) were to discover:

- student teachers' attitudes to Britain's cooperation with other European countries
- student teachers' attitudes to Britain's closer integration with other European countries
- student teachers' attitudes to the European dimension in education
- to what extent student teachers had been able to consider the European dimension in their training course
- if student teachers intended to include a European dimension in their future teaching.

In sections one, two and three, respondents were invited to agree or disagree with statements on a five-point scale, namely: strongly agree, agree, no opinion, disagree and strongly disagree. In sections four and five, there was a mixture of questions requiring a yes/no response and those of an open-ended nature, inviting lengthier comments. For the purposes of this study, the students were asked to consider Europe in its wider geographical context and not just Europe as defined by the EC. The questionnaire yielded both quantitative and qualitative data. The quantitative data has been analysed in terms of the independent variables of age, gender, subject specialism and whether or not the students were future teachers of modern languages (linguists/non-linguists). It was felt that this latter variable was significant because a large majority of the students following the PGCE in modern languages would have spent a year abroad as part of their undergraduate study and it might be worthwhile to investigate whether they expressed more positive views about European awareness than the other students.

THE SAMPLE

In terms of gender, males made up 33.3 per cent of the sample and females 66.7 per cent (as opposed to 38.8 per cent males and 61.2 per cent females in the whole course), so a slightly higher proportion of females responded to the questionnaire. The ages of the students in the sample ranged from 20 to 47 and were analysed in three bands as is shown in Table 5.1.

Table 5.1   *Breakdown of student ages in percentages*

Age band	% of student sample
20–23	52
24–29	30
30+	18

The percentages of students following the different subject methods are shown in Table 5.2, and are comparable with the percentages of students in each subject method on the whole course:

Table 5.2   *Breakdown of student method subjects on PGCE course in percentages*

Subject	% of student sample
Science	20.2
Mathematics	19.4
Modern Languages	19.3
English	18.6
Geography	10.1
History	9.3
Classics	3.1
Total	100.0

Thus, in terms of subject specialism, the sample consisted of 19.3 per cent of linguists and 80.7 per cent of non-linguists (those students not studying a foreign language as a teaching subject).

SUMMARY OF EMPIRICAL DATA

Section 1: Britain cooperating with other European countries

This first group of statements was partly intended to set the students' perception of their own intentions to teach about or through Europe against their view of how they see Britain should work with Europe in different socio-political spheres. The normal assumption would be that teachers' desires to promote Europe in school is backed by a parallel positive view on national cooperation with Europe. The data for Section 1 reveals that the majority of student teachers are positive in matters of cooperation between Britain and other European countries. Figure 5.1 shows that the students were very positive in terms of political and economic cooperation, and still positive, though slightly less so, with regard to social legislation and cultural cooperation.

It is interesting that the students are slightly more positive in terms of political, economic and social legislation cooperation than in the area of cultural cooperation. One might have predicted that it would be the other way round. It is perhaps encouraging that the students are so positive in terms of political cooperation in the context of the ongoing 'eurosquabbles' on the political front in the UK. On the other hand, in the light of the discussion of social psychological studies of attitudes to Europe in Chapter 2, one might interpret this response as a preference between 'utilitarian' and 'affective'

Figure 5.1 *Positive responses of student teachers in matters of cooperation between Britain and other European countries*

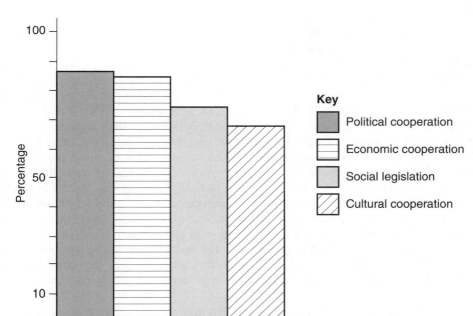

modes of support. Utilitarian support, represented by cooperation in areas of political, economic and social policy may be perceived as being beneficial to Britain, whereas affective support, represented by cultural cooperation, might impinge on cultural or national identities.

With regard to the independent variables of age and linguists/non-linguists, no significance was evident, but gender, however, was found to have been a significant factor in the areas of economic and cultural cooperation. In both areas, male student teachers were more strongly in agreement than their female counterparts. 42 per cent of males were strongly in agreement with economic cooperation as against 20 per cent of females, and 41 per cent of males were strongly in agreement with cultural cooperation compared with 31 per cent of females. A higher percentage of female students (22 per cent) also disagreed or strongly disagreed with cultural cooperation compared with 14 per cent of males. It is difficult to see a reason for this gender bias, especially in the case of cultural cooperation, unless one takes a more traditional, stereotypical view that economics is a 'male' domain with strong male role models, but that reasoning cannot be applied to the area of political cooperation, where gender is not a significant factor. In terms of subject specialism breakdown, this was only found to be of significance in the area of economic cooperation, where the mathematics students were more strongly in agreement (50 per cent) than their peers. This could again be explained in a utilitarian way, since mathematics would play an important part in economic cooperation.

Section 2: Britain bringing practices into line with other European countries

In this section the general spheres referred to previously are honed down to more specific issues of legislation. Further, while the statements in Section 1 imply an acceptance of cooperation on an equal basis with Europe, those in this Section 2 were framed in such a way as to indicate the extent to which the students accept the idea of Britain deferring to a greater European communal authority. The phrase 'bringing practices into line with' here implies that it is Europe which is setting the agenda for change and legislation. It is striking that in the section which asks whether or not Britain should bring its practices into line with other European countries, student teachers are more guarded in their responses. Figure 5.2 shows the percentage responses of those agreeing or strongly agreeing to be generally lower, with the exception of equal opportunities legislation, than those in Section 1. In other words, cooperation between Britain and other European countries is warmly welcomed, but anything requiring Britain to change its practices or to concede ground is greeted more cautiously. Figure 5.2 shows clearly that student teachers are less in favour of changing practices in the areas of health/national insurance, electoral systems and legal systems than they are in the areas of educational qualifications, employment laws and equal opportunities legislation. This could be due to a lack of knowledge of the former areas in other European countries and a greater familiarity with the latter three, or a suspicion or fear that health, elec-

Figure 5.2   *Positive responses of student teachers in matters concerning Britain bringing certain practices into line with other European countries*

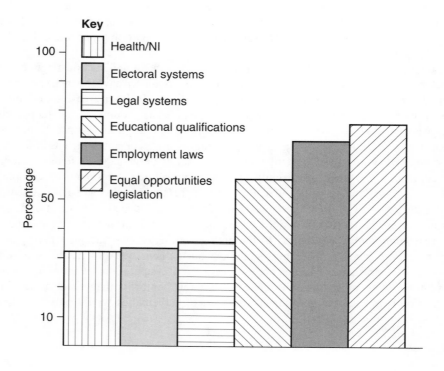

toral and legal systems in other countries may not be as good as in Britain. This surmise is not backed up by any evidence, however.

As well as the more muted response to the idea of changing practices, significant groups of students had no opinion in these areas, ranging from 29.5 per cent who had no opinion in the area of the legal system to 13.2 per cent who had no opinion in the area of equal opportunities legislation. Again, this could reflect a lack of knowledge or understanding of other countries' systems rather than an indifference to the questions.

The variables of gender, age and linguists/non-linguists were only significant in limited areas in this section. The linguists/non-linguists variable was very significant in the area of educational qualifications, with 72 per cent of linguists being in agreement with the statement compared with 52.3 per cent of non-linguists, and an emphatic 48 per cent of the linguists being strongly in agreement as opposed to only 13.3 per cent of the non-linguists. This was perhaps a predictable picture, since the linguists may well have spent a prolonged period of residence in another European country, and would value the benefits, in terms of employment and job opportunities, of having some kind of mutual recognition of educational qualifications. Gender proved to be a very significant variable and age was significant in the area of equal opportunities legislation. A high 82.6 per cent of females agreed with the statement that Britain should bring its own practices into line with other European countries compared with only 57.1 per cent of the males. At the other end of the scale, 26.1 per cent of males disagreed with the statement as opposed to only 5.9 per cent of females. An explanation here is that women perceive the area of equal opportunities as much more important than do men, in that much of the equal opportunities legislation over the recent past has involved giving women the same opportunities as men already had. Age, on the other hand, presented a slightly more complicated picture, as can be seen in Table 5.3.

Table 5.3 *Comparison of different age groups' responses to statement: 'Britain should bring its own practices into line with other European countries with regard to equal opportunities legislation'*

Age group	Agree %	Disagree %	No opinion %
20–23	82.3	5.9	11.8
24–29	60.5	29	10.5
30+	73.9	4.4	21.7

Students in the youngest age group came out much more strongly in support of the statement, followed by those in the oldest age group. One explanation of this finding could be that students in the youngest age group have only relatively recently completed their secondary education, and it is quite likely that they had experience of equal opportunities policies in operation in schools. Similarly, students in the oldest age group may have experienced equal opportunities issues in previous employment and age and experience combined may have led them to value such legislation more highly, say, than the students in the 24–29 age band. It is interesting to note at this point that in the whole of the questionnaire, in which there were 26 questions, or parts of questions, age was only shown to be a significant variable in the question on equal opportunities legislation. In all the other questions, age did not play a significant part in the way the student teachers responded.

Section 3: Education and the European dimension

The statements here were intended to indicate the student teachers' attitudes to different ways of promoting the European dimension in schools. Student teachers gave their most positive answers in this section and there was considerable agreement in response to all the statements, as shown in Figure 5.3.

Figure 5.3   *Positive responses of student teachers in relation to European educational issues*

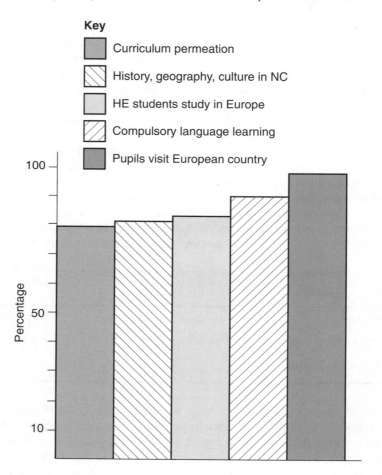

Key

- Curriculum permeation
- History, geography, culture in NC
- HE students study in Europe
- Compulsory language learning
- Pupils visit European country

There was almost complete consensus of opinion (96.9 per cent) that all British pupils should have the opportunity to visit another European country, and compulsory foreign-language learning was also strongly supported (89.1 per cent). It is encouraging that all student teachers in the sample appear to hold such positive attitudes to education and the European dimension and, perhaps, one could feel optimistic that a group of future teachers demonstrates such a commitment. These very positive attitudes contrast with those displayed in the previous section. Perhaps the student teachers are able to separate the education issues of Europe from other more contentious issues, such as the political, social and economic ones, for example.

The independent variables of gender and linguists/non-linguists played a small part in this section. Gender was a significant element in the responses to the statement that 'European awareness should permeate all subjects in the curriculum', with a high 87.2 per cent of females agreeing compared with 62.8 per cent of males. Furthermore, 18.6 per cent of males had no opinion on the statement, and 18.6 per cent disagreed with it. Clearly, females see European awareness as an important addition to the curriculum, whereas males feel more ambivalent. It is difficult to offer a reasonable explanation here, but it certainly reinforces the findings of the main CRMLE research, where the female pupils were found to be more strongly pro-European than the male pupils. In addition, the linguist/non-linguist variable was found to be significant in this statement too, with an expectedly high 92 per cent of linguists supporting the statement compared with 76.2 per cent of non-linguists. One does not have to look far for an explanation here, since the European dimension is already an integral part of the curriculum for linguists. Gender also played a significant role in the responses to the statement that 'All British students in HE should have the opportunity to study for part of their course in another European country.' Although males (81.4 per cent) and females (82.6 per cent) were almost in equal agreement, the females (41.9 per cent) agreed more strongly than the males (18.6 per cent). As the majority of linguists in HE is usually female, this would reinforce the result here. As it has already been stated earlier in this chapter that spending a year abroad is in most cases part of a linguist's undergraduate experience, there is nothing surprising in the fact that linguists (88 per cent) agreed more strongly than non-linguists (51.4 per cent) that 'All British pupils should have the opportunity to visit another European country.' What is encouraging from Table 5.4 is the almost total agreement with the statement by all students.

Table 5.4　*Degrees of agreement between linguists and non-linguists on pupils visiting other European countries*

	Strongly agree %	Agree %
Linguists	88	12
Non-linguists	51.4	44.8

Section 4: The European dimension in a PGCE course at the University of Nottingham

In this section, student teachers were asked to consider the role of the European dimension within their own training course, the specific elements within the course, both school-based and institution-based, and they were then encouraged to comment at greater length if they had included any aspect of the European dimension in their own teaching during teaching practice. The aim of these questions was to discover to what extent student teachers felt that they had experienced the European dimension in the university-based part of the course, and if they had then followed it up in a practical way in the school-based part.

Course Structure

At this point, it is worth considering the structure of the specific PGCE course in question and the way in which the European dimension is handled in order to understand the context of the student teachers' responses afterwards. The European dimension is perceived as a dimension in National Curriculum terms in that it is supposed to permeate the whole curriculum. It is not intended to be seen as a separate element. It is first introduced as an element within the educational studies work on multiculturalism and students also have the opportunity of choosing it as a topic for the assessed essay. The European dimension may also be considered during subject method work, and not surprisingly there are some method areas where it is given greater prominence than in others. Student teachers may also meet the European dimension during their practical work in schools, which in this case study consists of three weeks of primary experience, one day a week in a secondary school in the autumn term, a full-time twelve-week teaching practice in the spring term and some further action-research based work in schools in the summer term. The department also takes part in a well-established ERASMUS network, having partners in five other European countries, following student and staff mobility programmes. During the summer term of 1994, nine ERASMUS students were received by the PGCE course from Vienna, Osnabrück and Nancy, and they were able to work alongside British students in method work and school-based work. Additionally, during the two week period of short courses at the end of the course, the European dimension was made the focus of a Europe Day, in which a visiting speaker from a neighbouring institution shared a one-hour lecture slot with a member of the department. The lecture covered the development of the European dimension and its place in the National Curriculum and the notion of a multicultural Europe of the regions. Student teachers then had the opportunity to meet in discussion groups for a workshop which included a cross-curricular planning activity and other tasks. Finally, there were two further short courses with a European dimension: 'Eurolink' (to the Channel Tunnel Exhibition Centre, Folkestone and Boulogne) was aimed to give students the opportunity to organize and experience a cross-curricular, educational visit and a 'World War One Battlefield Tour', which formed an introduction to touring the Western Front with students of all ages, working in cross-curricular ways and looking at PSE and the European movement.

What student teachers said about their course

An encouraging 92.3 per cent said they had had the opportunity to consider the European dimension during the PGCE course. However, when asked to consider the various elements of the course separately, the responses varied considerably, as is shown in Figure 5.4.

This is not as positive as it might seem when the subject variable is taken into account. Subject is a very significant factor in all the elements shown, with the exception of the educational studies work, where 75.4 per cent of the students said they had been able to consider the European dimension.

In subject method work, 49.6 per cent of the students answered that they had considered the European dimension, but significantly more linguists (88 per cent) and geographers (84.6 per cent) had considered it than other subject areas. In English and

Figure 5.4   *Student teachers' experiences of the European dimension during the PGCE course*

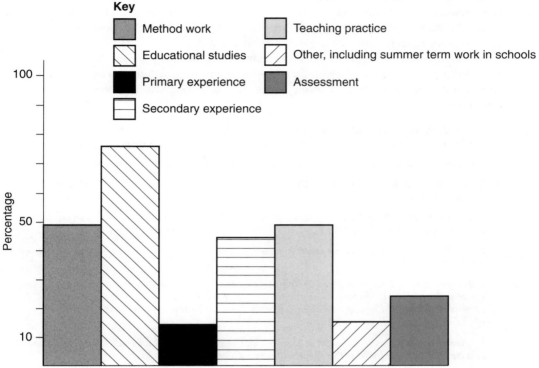

mathematics, for example, 75 per cent and 76 per cent of students respectively said that they had not been able to consider the European dimension in relation to their teaching subjects. In all other areas of the course, it was significant that more linguists had had the opportunity to consider the European dimension than non-linguists, especially during the primary teaching experience, the summer term work in schools and as part of the assessed work. However, when commenting on the autumn term school experience and the spring term block teaching practice, a slightly different picture emerges, as is shown in Table 5.5.

Table 5.5   *Percentages of students from different subject areas incorporating a European dimension in their school-based work*

Subject	Autumn term teaching experience %	Spring term teaching practice %
English	25	20.8
Mathematics	12	25
Science	26.9	23.1
Geography	76.9	83.3
History	58.3	66.7
Classics	75	100
Modern Languages	84	91.7

It is evident that in geography, history, classics and modern languages significantly more students were able to incorporate a European dimension than did those in English, mathematics and science. This reflects the pattern which emerged from the CRMLE research, where the pupils revealed that the subjects in which they learned most about Europe were modern languages, geography and history.

As can be seen in Figure 5.4, 48 per cent of the student teachers said that they had included aspects of the European dimension in their own teaching during teaching practice. They were then asked to specify what they had done. Here follows a selection of their comments:

We analysed an Italian advert in English (for media advertising) with year 10, and considered Italian culture in our eyes and in the advert. (English)

Study and exploring effects of holocaust on families in Holland in Drama lessons. (English)

Conversion graphs – currency, distances, petrol usage. Looked at travelling abroad. Mapwork. (Maths)

Making it known about European mathematicians and used countries to demonstrate lesson on areas and percentages. (Maths)

Looking at telescopes and microscopes and researching about the European scientists involved. (Science)

Participated in a European week. Used flashcards in Year 7 history lessons for classroom commands spoken in French. Taught history in French (as far as possible) to Year 7. Looked at theme of English language link with Norman French. Made links wherever possible in all lessons, all years. (History)

I covered a topic on the EU with a Year 9 class, which included an individual study of the culture and geography of a European country. (Geography)

Effect of national identity e.g. Italy. (Geography)

Roman occupation and influence over Europe – unifying attitudes and ways of life bringing cooperation to many tribes. (Classics)

Classics is the European subject in terms of language, geography, history, literature and politics. (Classics)

Introduction of European geography and names of countries in MFL – examination of cultural differences. (Modern Languages)

In French and German lessons – where the languages are spoken, multiculturalism of those countries, political background with history. (Modern Languages)

It is encouraging that the students' comments covered the complete range of subjects offered on the PGCE course, and in approximately proportionate numbers. One might have expected that the majority of comments would come from the areas of history, geography and modern languages, given that these were the three subjects where the pupils in the CRMLE study said they gained most of their knowledge about Europe (Chapter 2), but this was not the case. Interesting ideas for introducing a European dimension came from students of English, maths, science and classics, too. Some of the examples are to do with knowledge and facts about Europe, but the themes of empathy, identity, multicultural Europe, Europe's position within the world and the teaching of other subjects through the medium of the foreign language are all mentioned. These ideas reflect some of the definitions and official guidelines on the European dimension which were reviewed in Chapter 1. This is encouraging, since the student teachers had probably not had exposure to such a wide range of literature and many of their ideas must have been self-generated.

When the students were asked if they understood the position of the European dimension within the National Curriculum, the following picture emerged (see Figure 5.5). Almost half the student teachers were confident that they understood the position of the European dimension in the National Curriculum, but a similar number felt uncertain or not at all sure. This may reflect the ambivalent attitude on the part of the DFEE and the absence of any curriculum guidance, as has already been commented upon in Chapter 3.

Figure 5.5 *Student teachers' understanding of the position of the European dimension within the National Curriculum*

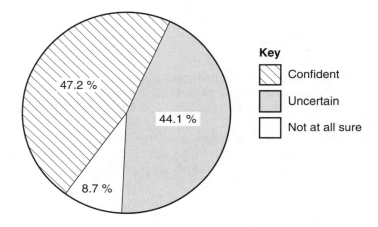

Section 5: The Future

In the final section of the questionnaire, student teachers were asked to what extent they intended to include any aspects of the European dimension in their future teaching, in order to assess what percentage of them thought they would, and to find out how they would do it. The results are shown in Figure 5.6.

The independent variables of gender and subject are important in this question, however. Taking the case of gender, a slightly higher percentage of females (30.5 per cent) than males (28.6 per cent) said they would incorporate aspects of the European dimension as a regular feature of their lessons, and a higher 69.5 per cent of females said they would do so occasionally compared with 61.9 per cent of males. Interestingly, no females said they did not intend to include a European dimension in their teaching, as opposed to 9.5 per cent of males who said they would not. This would appear to be further evidence that the European dimension does have a gender bias, and that females are generally more positive to European issues, certainly within an educational framework. Perhaps it is their perception that there are more possibilities for them in a European arena, and that equality of opportunity is more attainable. In terms of subject, linguists (78.3 per cent), geographers (63.6 per cent) and historians (41.7 per cent) all

Figure 5.6   *Pie chart to show if student teachers intend to include aspects of the European dimension in their future teaching*

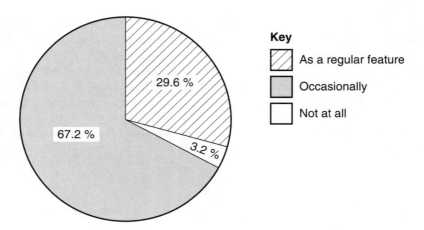

intended to include aspects of the European dimension in their future teaching as a regular feature and significant numbers of English students (87.5 per cent), mathematicians (75 per cent), scientists (100 per cent) and classicists (75 per cent) intended to include it occasionally.

Student teachers were asked to specify how they would include aspects of the European dimension in their future teaching, and some very interesting and creative suggestions were made, a selection of which are presented below.

i. Teaching about Europe for comparative purposes

Different objectives were apparent in the comparative methods suggested. In some cases, the European examples were intended to broaden the scope of the topic being taught; in others the aim was to learn from contrasts with the British context; and in others the aim was to identify influences.

> *Cultural background to literary works, works from other countries, issue work e.g. on bullying and racial stereotypes. (English)*

> *I intend to use European literature in lessons alongside English literature, as a comparison and to broaden. I also hope to use themes and issues which occur in 'English-based' classwork and encourage research on those in other European countries or European history e.g. Second World War poets. (English)*

> *Biology makes pupils aware of the range of different habitats/adaptations of animals and plants across Europe (conservation/ecology work). Other parts of science – bring as many recent European developments in science into lessons using* New Scientist *etc. Past inventions from Europe. (Science)*

> *One cannot escape including Europe in a Latin, ancient Greek or ancient history course. The classical civilisation course requires that modern Europe is directly compared to ancient. (Classics)*

ii. Illustrative references to Europe, not for comparative purposes

Here we have indications of the extent to which future British teachers are inclined to use Europe or European examples as a teaching resource. This would imply a more integrative function, since the pupils being taught in this way would have a more 'drip-feed' exposure to Europe, with less of a 'them and us' perspective to the presentation.

> *Perhaps by using statistics of various countries/populations etc. when doing work on percentages or other statistical work ... Perhaps exchange rates, calculating the cost of various holidays using a database. Calculating distances of journeys/time of travel etc. (Maths)*

> *Science has developed through the work of scientists worldwide but at KS3 basic concepts are European (Ampère, Volta, Ohm, Gauss etc.). Unfortunately, the historical aspect of the subject was lost in the first curriculum review and there is time only for a passing mention of common objectives. At A level, we should consider the consequences of modern scientific trends which are pan-European e.g. genetic engineering; effects of biotechnology on crop variety or pest control etc. (Science)*

> *Hope to use European examples wherever possible. Perhaps try original language texts with VI form. Extend themes to include Europe. Encourage visits abroad where possible. Hope to include Europe in PSE lessons on equal opportunities, environment, etc. (History)*

> *Geography ought really to be a global subject but with emphases on the UK and then Europe. It is important to use a wide variety of examples that are most appropriate and interesting. (Geography)*

iii. Participating in European projects

In these statements student teachers showed their commitment to teaching 'Europe through Europe'.

> *Through organising trips and exchanges to other European countries; language clubs, other links such as email, penpals; language festivals; theatre/cinema trips (European and other foreign films). (Modern Languages)*

> *In tandem with EIU, I think there are opportunities for linking up with DTI regional export centres to devise meaningful tasks for pupils of all ages. The opportunities offered by NVQ/GNVQ are particularly interesting in this respect. (Modern Languages)*

Students wrote at greater length and in more detail in response to this question than they did when asked about their teaching practice. Many of the ideas which had been used on teaching practice were repeated here, but there was also a selection of new and original thoughts. The idea of examining common issues across Europe is mentioned several times, as is cross-curricular language teaching. Linking with schools in other parts of Europe is also introduced, as is the idea of the European dimension being a part of PSE or tutorial time. Many students were concerned that a European dimension could conflict with the notion of multiculturalism, or a world approach to the curriculum, and were keen to stress that the European dimension was a part of a whole and not an end in itself.

With regard to their future careers, student teachers were asked whether they would consider seeking a teaching post in a European country other than Britain. A very high

71.1 per cent said that they would, while 28.9 per cent responded negatively. This large 'yes' group is interesting, in that it must include more than the linguists, which indicates that there is a group of students with language skills, or who do not regard the language issues as problematic, or both. Whatever the case, by working in another European country, these students would find themselves unable to avoid confronting European dimension issues, such as comparison of educational systems, language and communication, cultural similarities and differences and so on. They would, in fact, be experiencing the European dimension in Europe, as referred to in Chapter 1, when Stobart's view of in, about and for Europe was discussed.

CASE STUDY CONCLUSIONS

It would be a mistake to claim significant conclusions from a small case study such as the one described in this chapter. It is possible, however, to draw some tentative conclusions which would be worthy of further investigation, and which might indicate some areas for future development. Within the framework of this study, student teachers appear reasonably positive about European issues, especially in the educational domain. In terms of their own training, students of modern languages, geography, history and classics appear to have had good opportunities for considering the European dimension, whereas students of English, mathematics and science do not. As for the future, it is encouraging that almost all the students would consider incorporating a European dimension in their teaching occasionally, and that some would do it on a more regular basis. Certainly, the practical teaching ideas suggested by the students are both imaginative and appropriate, and would make the understanding of the European dimension for the pupils more approachable and relevant. It may well be that a 'bottom-up' approach will be more successful if the next generation of teachers can put into practice some of their ideas. Courses of initial teacher education should also take into account the needs of all students to be able to consider the European dimension during their training.

INITIAL TEACHER TRAINING AND THE EUROPEAN DIMENSION

As can be seen from the case study, many student teachers are indeed enthusiastic and optimistic about integrating aspects of the European dimension in their future teaching, even if teaching something other than modern languages. Indeed some may be quite ambitious and innovative in their intentions. It is important to stress that this survey of the student teachers occurred before radical reforms to teacher training had taken effect. To what extent is their training in both higher education institutions and partnership schools likely to prepare them now for this task? How has the government made it easier for their training institutions to facilitate such a development in recent legislation?

Following the Education Reform Act of 1988, a circular was issued by the Department of Education and Science which dealt specifically with the initial training of both student and articled teachers. Circular 24/89 specified the accreditation criteria for courses of initial teacher training and included the requirements that they should develop in student and articled teachers:

(awareness of) the links and common ground between subjects and (the ability to) incorporate in their teaching cross-curricular dimensions (eg. equal opportunities, multicultural education and personal and social education), themes (eg. environmental education, economic and industrial understanding, health education and *the European dimension in education)* and skills (oracy, literacy and numeracy). (Our emphasis)

These cross-curricular dimensions, themes and skills were included in the Whole Curriculum document published by the National Curriculum Council (1990) to be taught across the ability range to all pupils. This laudable aim was never fully realized and when the full impact of the implementation of the National Curriculum was understood they were quickly dropped. There was hardly enough time and space for all the statutory core and foundation subjects and their concomitant assessment on the timetable let alone any extra cross-curricular issues.

However, the circular did acknowledge the importance of the European dimension for prospective teachers in training and it was only three years later that even this slight reference was removed. In 1992 the government moved towards a school-based approach to teacher training and deleted any reference to the European dimension.

The Department for Education Circular 9/92 on Initial Teacher Training does not contain any reference to the European dimension other than obliquely under 'Further Professional Development' where it states that :

- Newly qualified teachers should have acquired in initial training the necessary foundation to develop:
- an understanding of the school as an institution and its place within the community (section 2.6.1)
- an awareness of individual differences, including social, psychological, developmental and cultural dimensions (section 2.6.4).

Since September 1994 all postgraduate teachers in training spend at least two-thirds of their time in a host school and only one-third in a Higher Education Institution.

The European dimension does not form a statutory part of the National Curriculum and is not mentioned in the final orders for modern foreign languages.

Traditionally modern languages departments have often been seen as the place with the responsibility for introducing the European dimension into the school, and yet the lack of formal emphasis upon the subject in the National Curriculum is a serious handicap in its dissemination. Without the requirement to include it for purposes of assessment or for OFSTED inspection, many teachers may not see it as a priority. This is indeed a problem for all cross-curricular teaching. Who has ownership and who monitors the delivery? Teachers who may be involved in delivering the European dimension may also be involved in inducting newly qualified teachers and mentoring trainee teachers.

Many trainee teachers of all subjects at both primary and secondary level now have less traditional backgrounds when they begin a PGCE course. For example, in place of moving straight from a first degree into a one-year training course, mature students may have moved into teaching from other employment or after having raised a family, or they may be native speakers for modern languages courses who have decided to settle in the UK, or students with combined degrees.

Many trainees also do not feel competent to teach the European dimension because of the perceived lack of their own basic knowledge and ambivalent feelings about Europe. They feel uncomfortable when straying outside the bounds of their own subject specialism. Some modern languages student teachers in particular may also have mixed feelings themselves about their own identity and nationality, especially those from Latin America who are intending to teach Spanish or who are from an ethnic minority in the UK.

This is the current context in which teachers of the future are being trained. Why should we continue to insist upon some form of training in approaches to the European dimension for student teachers? Where should that training take place? Can it form part of the profile of a newly qualified teacher? There could be grades of expertise to which new entrants to the profession could aspire in the realm of the European dimension. For example: European dimension coordinator, administrator of exchanges, European projects supervisor. This approach may also have the added benefit that teachers would have ownership of the process and thereby be more committed.

Data from the other countries in the European Union involved in the CRMLE research show that there is considerable variety in initial teacher training. Research from the European Commission itself (1995) reports the following findings (based on evidence collected in 1991/92, it has been amended to reflect the changes in England). In Spain and France initial teacher training for all levels of education is provided in universities. For the later stages of education, university training is the general rule in the member states with the Netherlands requiring some non-university training for upper secondary teachers and England following the school-based training model with links to higher education.

The following extract from the European Commission (1995a) report shows clearly the distinction in training patterns for teachers of different levels:

> In the Member States of the European Union, the professional and practical training courses for teachers are provided either at the same time as their general (degree) course – the concurrent model – or following the general course, for instance at post-graduate level – the consecutive model.
>
> The concurrent model is more common in training for nursery and primary teaching. Conversely the consecutive model is more typical of initial training for secondary teaching. Thus as the proportion of professional and practical training in initial training courses diminishes, the higher the level for which the intending teacher is training.

If there is a difficulty as to where to place the European dimension on the school timetable, there is an even more pressing issue as to where to place it in the initial teacher training phase. There is much variety, as can be seen above, in the ways in which different member states tackle the professional training and development of their teachers. For the European dimension to become a reality in the lives of all participants in the education process (teachers, pupils, parents), then those who make decisions about curricula content will need to give it greater weight and emphasis.

Evidence from the research shows that pupils would very much like to be better informed about the European dimension and that they would like the schools to help them interpret the data that comes in from the media. Evidence from Chapter 3 also shows an almost complete lack of in-service training for teachers on the topic of the European dimension. If the new entrants to the profession are not fired with enthusiasm about the topic and willing to present it to the pupils, then who will be?

Schools need strategies, policies and funding to enable them to move forward in the area of the European dimension. If there is no political will from senior management and the governors in this area then it will fail. It needs backing from the top. Heads of department also need training in how to present the European dimension and how to integrate it into their existing schemes of study.

It is significant that 1996 has been designated 'European Year of Lifelong Learning' by the European Commission. The project's aim is to promote 'personal development of individuals and their integration into working life and society' through lifelong learning (European Commission, 1995). The European Commission is promoting this Year in a number of ways. The official launch was in Venice during the Italian European presidency and the UK launch took place in Edinburgh on 22 February 1996. There are many strands to this Year, in common with many European initiatives. Among them are high quality general education, continuing education and training, links between education and training providers and business and significantly in the context of this book: development of the European dimension of initial and continuing education and training.

The notion of lifelong (or lifetime) learning is being taken up increasingly by schools and others with initiatives such as Investors in People. The idea is that every employee (and in our context that means every teacher) has a responsibility to further their own learning through involvement in continuing professional development. In the DFEE consultation document 'Lifetime Learning' (Crown Copyright, 1995) there is the following paragraph:

> Lifetime learning also plays a key part in our wider social and cultural activity, yielding benefits extending beyond the economic field. The preservation and acquisition of knowledge and the ability of individuals to fulfil their personal capacity to learn are vital signs of a free and civilised society.

Individual teachers need to see the relevance and practical possibilities afforded to them by being involved in the European dimension. This is as much for job satisfaction and personal development as for career advancement. This also includes the possibility of fulfilment of that personal capacity referred to earlier. Self-fulfilment can include being involved with something bigger than or even outside of oneself.

Schools could be encouraged to see where they were in terms of promoting the European dimension (however they themselves defined that) on a possible five-point scale. This scale is a modified version of the one produced by the National Council for Educational Technology for the implementation of Information Technology in modern languages (1995, p. 8):

Promoting the European dimension across the whole school curriculum

(Stage 1) Localized:	a few teachers do a little on their own initiative; mainly reactive.
(Stage 2) Co-ordinated:	some curriculum development in place; strategic policies.
(Stage 3) Transformative:	most teachers recognize and value need for teaching ED integrated policy.
(Stage 4) Embedded:	regular review cycle; higher order skills; informs curriculum planning.
(Stage 5) Innovative:	strategic commitment to ED in learning; staff training/ demand-led.

Another way of demonstrating that degree of increasing involvement is as follows:

> INDIVIDUAL
> COLLABORATIVE
> COMMITTED
> INTUITIVE
> INFLUENTIAL

By attending in-service training or on their own school-based training days schools could see how they were to reach the next step of involvement in the European dimension. If fairly localized and carried along by the enthusiasm of one or two teachers, they would try to take one step forward to 'Co-ordinated' and endeavour to involve some more staff and write some ideas into their curriculum time, especially that precious time handed back to them by the Dearing review in 1995.

What has all this to do with initial teacher training? Unless there is already in place in schools a framework into which student teachers can fit, then it is unlikely that much progress can be made. Of course some newly qualified teachers do become the vanguard of innovation and stimulate departments to take on new ideas. However this is more likely to be successful if there is already fertile ground for ideas to be planted in, otherwise it can be a lonely and frustrating task. Synergy tends to flourish where committed people empower their peers and subordinates to develop their strengths and thus contribute greatly to the task in hand.

During the twelve weeks spent at the higher education institution some progress can be made towards updating and increasing knowledge of Europe, learning strategies for imparting such knowledge and carrying out research into successful schemes elsewhere. However this is of necessity only a small part of the training programme. Because the bulk of it takes place in school, the bulk of the concentration on the European dimension also needs to take place in school and that needs to be planned, co-ordinated and implemented. Ideally where there are proactive partnerships between the training providers, then there could be some fruitful collaboration on such an issue. This could also form a useful project for any head of department or other teacher seriously considering further training as a mentor or preparing a module in a higher degree. In order for this to be more than just tinkering around the edges and paying lip-service to the whole notion, there would have to be a fundamental investment of commitment by the training institutions to the whole project.

It is very tempting to think that this is just another initiative with which to bombard teachers when they are already suffering from initiative overload. Why give them something else to worry about when they are more concerned with league tables, exam success, OFSTED inspections and other more pressing demands?

Student teachers may not also perceive this as a priority either because the schools where they are being trained also may not see it as a priority, or because they are principally and rightly concerned about their own classroom performance and want to establish themselves before launching on some new initiative. Awareness of their own lack of expertise may also act as an obstacle. However this is precisely where the third part of the equation, the higher education institutions, can help. Partnerships between institutions ought to mean just that: each contributing its own strengths so that the whole is greater than the sum of the parts. Because of their perceived expertise in the field and their probable links with other HEIs elsewhere in Europe, they are in a very good position to offer advice, training and openings to funding that schools may not be in a position to access.

HEIs may also have a number of EU students (ERASMUS and other) who would probably be very willing to become involved in just such a project and visit schools in order to present up-to-date information to school pupils. Their very presence would signal to pupils and teachers alike the existence and importance of other communities and cultures not so far from them and from whom they could learn so much.

It has to be admitted that the present arrangements for initial teacher training do not present a very optimistic scenario in which development of the European dimension is likely to take place. However, when teacher training is seen in a much broader light and encompasses much more than a one-year introductory course, then it is possible to see some future strategies. Initial training is just the first step in an on-going process of personal and professional development. If during that first year some interest in the topic of the European dimension can be awakened, then maybe that is all that can be reasonably expected, given that student teachers have many other pressing concerns upon them. As long as that awakening is then given a further boost by imaginative involvement in their first destination school and as long as the European dimension is included in that list of desirables that have parity of esteem with other matters such as information technology or vocational qualifications, then progress can be made.

In the end it is a matter of political will. Do we want a teaching profession that is able to take its place with all other European countries in developing citizenship and political maturity among its pupils or do we want to stand outside and not even join the debate?

Conclusion

At the heart of the current search for a European identity is the interrelationship between the geographical boundaries of the land mass, the political status of the Union and the multicultural and multi-ethnic nature of its constituents. The principle which underpins the European dimension in education is the need to help young people explore and understand the interrelationship. We propose that this should be part of their entitlement curriculum. We do not propose this notion lightly. The economic and socio-political changes now occurring (and likely to accelerate over the next ten years) are so fundamental that all youngsters will be affected by them. We are not dealing here with differences of shades of political opinion. The Single European Act and the Treaty of Maastricht were thresholds that national governments agreed to step over. Once national frontiers and work restrictions as well as tariff barriers were removed, Europe became our children's inheritance. A parallel may be drawn with the status of information technology. National curricula have recognized that information technology is part of every young learners' future and that adults who provide education may not debar them from their entitlement to it. In exactly the same way national curricula should ensure that young people are not debarred from their opportunities, rights and obligations as European citizens.

The lasting significance of the 24 May Resolution is that it defines a set of achievable goals now to be, in part, addressed through programmes such as SOCRATES and LEONARDO. The power of these programmes is that they are cross-dimensional and process-oriented. The linguistic diversity of Europe, its economic potential and its cultural mosaic is to be accessed not through a 'top-down' transference of knowledge but by parallel exploration and *ouverture* in a number of educational domains: school children, students in higher education, trainee teachers, teachers, teacher trainers and other experts in the field of education. These European citizens will need first-hand contact and informed reflection to understand fully the humanist ideals of the community and the global perspective in which the Union will operate. We have seen that, although individual governments' official responses to the Resolution were detailed and positive, there is little evidence, eight years on, of coherent implementation. The UK government, in particular, has diluted the propelling fuel of the resolution such that implementation is fragmented even if excellent local initiatives are to be found. The difficulty is that we have yet to understand fully how the EU will 'support and supplement the actions of member states', (see Appendix E1). A typical example of this is primary foreign-language provision in England and Wales where clearly European Union momentum is not sufficient to supplement a lack of conviction at the national political level.

The CRMLE research project has discovered a mismatch between the claimed provision of education systems and young people's perceptions of what they are receiving. This is in conflict with their expectations. On the one hand some teachers and head-teachers have been able to outline where in their curriculum Europe is studied. On the other hand we have been made aware of learners' perceptions that they do not really know enough or understand the complexities of Europe. Why should this mismatch have occurred? The answers are probably as varied as the number of educational systems which the Union encompasses. Nevertheless some general themes emerge. First, adults control the content, the discourse and the presentation of Europe. It is not surprising therefore that young people should feel excluded. Second, the delivery of all matters European through what are essentially content subjects such as history, geography and modern languages is in stark contrast with the dynamic processes which youngsters experience through the media's presentation of European policy. There is thus an interplay between formal education and the media's non-formal education. However they have difficulty in assessing meaning from the media. Moreover content is much more difficult to challenge than policy and yet content affects lives much less than policy. Beyond the classroom, on their television screens and in their newspapers, youngsters have the sensation that their future is being decided for them and we have heard in countless interviews that the media is unable to 'mediate' the complexities of the issues. As researchers we were both astonished and privileged to experience the pleasure which young people felt, particularly in schools in mainland Europe, at being consulted. In Chapter 4 we have proposed a basis for a more dynamic and participative learning process which will involve and motivate pupils better.

Educators in the European Union need to be aware of a number of other conclusions which the project data suggests. Females, whites, the better off and those who have travelled more were in a better position to understand and seize the opportunities which greater openness and integration have to offer. It is vital that the social exclusion being experienced at regional and national levels is not reinforced by educational opportunities emanating from the European Union.

Young people also recognized that a form of exclusion could occur through economically strong nations in the EU having hegemony over weaker ones. This is an issue which in recent years has begun to be addressed by Brussels through, for instance, its greater promotion of the least taught languages of the Union. An understanding of this principle is vital and should form part of the European dimension in education. The last six decades of the twentieth century have seen the total rejection and break-up of colonialism as much due to its imposition of one language and culture as its political and military subjugation of one people over others. The resulting trend has been towards smaller and smaller 'national' units often defining themselves by the minutest of religious or cultural differences with, in some cases, disastrous consequences. The coming together of nations in Europe has begun to reverse that trend. It is a delicate and tenuous permission granted by the peoples of one nation in that they are prepared, in part, to be governed by others. That permission will only be granted if they are assured that their different cultures, languages and allegiances are recognized as having equal worth. The multiple identities and the more complex attachments which this cooperation between nations will necessitate will not be enhanced by the consolidation of what French educators refer to as *le tunnel tout anglais*. Moreover it is vital that the European dimension be firmly placed in a wider global context, recognizing and valuing the relationships which Europe has both with the countries of origin of its multicultural citizens and recognizing the cultural wealth which the citizens themselves have brought to the Union.

Throughout this book we have discovered that there are, as far as we can tell, no human barriers to a greater visibility of the European dimension in education. Pupils, teachers and headteachers have all, by and large, responded positively. We have noted that in England governing bodies, those with ultimate responsibility for the curriculum, see no need to oppose education for European citizenship on the grounds of political indoctrination. In fact many see a contradiction between the educational imperatives of Europe and the lack of knowledge about European issues deriving from a narrow curriculum. They believe young people should be encouraged to explore the shifting sands of their belonging. Indeed school is a safe place to examine the differences between nation and state, between personal and social identity. The European dimension in the curriculum, these governors believe, should reflect the balance which is being sought between the challenge of the free trade markets and the challenge of multiculturalism.

We have explored the relationships between identity and citizenship. We have suggested that the latter is bestowed by institutions on individuals, the former is chosen freely by individuals from the multiple identities available to them in the modern world. Nevertheless being at ease with a double or even triple identity may well allow individuals to operate more efficiently in the increasingly intercultural nature of the European context. English pupils, more than others, may need to have this proposal put to them and schools and the media have an enormous role to play in providing a European balance to the diet of Anglo-American culture.

The tentative model we have proposed for the European dimension in education attempts to harness more efficiently the forces at play and the needs manifesting themselves in the few remaining years of this millennium: that is, the devaluation of knowledge in favour of the upgrading of understanding and skills. It also mirrors more accurately the cyclic nature of self-development for teachers through reflective practice. Do we then need some standardization across Europe of the basic competencies we should expect from our future workforce? This is a fruitful area for further research. One thing is clear: greater mobility of the European teaching force will not come about without some harmonization of basic teaching competencies. In turn, mobility is inextricably linked to diversification of language provision, to the celebration of other cultures, to peaceful co-existence and to integration within the Union. We have seen that teachers in training also regard positively their European future and want to play their part in the shaping of a European identity. This will translate itself into a consistent determination, as informed and discriminating decision-makers, to match their personal needs to the constantly developing and broadening educational context. This openness to change will infuse our schools with the understanding that education is for life and lifelong learning is not only about personal fulfilment but also about understanding oneself.

Appendices

A1: CRMLE Pupil questionnaire: survey of young people's attitudes to Europe

Suggested time for completion of questionnaire: 30 minutes

01 Country...........................

02 Town...........................

03 School/college.......................

04 Age...............

05 Male [ ]   Female [ ]

06 Would you describe yourself as:
    [ ] Afro-Caribbean   [ ] Asian   [ ] White   [ ] Other

07 Occupation of parent(s) or guardian(s)..

08 Have you ever been to another European country?   [ ]yes   [ ]no
    If yes, which one(s)...
    was this/were these with   family [ ]   [ ]   [ ]   [ ]   [ ]   (tick one box
                                 friends [ ]   [ ]   [ ]   [ ]   [ ]   per visit)
                                 school [ ]   [ ]   [ ]   [ ]   [ ]

09 How well informed do you think you are about Europe?:
    (please tick *one* of the boxes)
    I am ...
    very well informed   [ ]
    quite well informed   [ ]
    not well informed   [ ]
    not at all informed   [ ]

Where do you get your knowledge about Europe from? State how much from each of the following:

10	from school?	[ ] all	[ ] most	[ ] a little	[ ] none
11	from home?	[ ] all	[ ] most	[ ] a little	[ ] none
12	from the media?	[ ] all	[ ] most	[ ] a little	[ ] none
13	from friends?	[ ] all	[ ] most	[ ] a little	[ ] none
14	from travel?	[ ] all	[ ] most	[ ] a little	[ ] none
15	from relatives or friends abroad?	[ ]all	[ ]most	[ ]a little	[ ]none

16   I get my
knowledge about Europe from other sources   [ ]true   [ ]untrue
If *true* please state which sources...

17   How often would you say you gained knowledge or understanding about Europe *in school*?
Please tick one of the following:
daily [ ]
a few lessons a week [ ]
once a week [ ]
once every few weeks [ ]
a few times a term [ ]
once a term [ ]
never or almost never [ ]
don't know [ ]

18   How much knowledge or understanding about Europe do you gain from each of the following subjects?

English	[ ] a lot	[ ] some	[ ] a little	[ ] none
Geography	[ ] a lot	[ ] some	[ ] a little	[ ] none
History	[ ] a lot	[ ] some	[ ] a little	[ ] none
Mathematics	[ ] a lot	[ ] some	[ ] a little	[ ] none
Modern Languages	[ ] a lot	[ ] some	[ ] a little	[ ] none
Science	[ ] a lot	[ ] some	[ ] a little	[ ] none
Sport/PE	[ ] a lot	[ ] some	[ ] a little	[ ] none
other subjects:	[ ] a lot	[ ] some	[ ] a little	[ ] none

19   What languages have you been taught at school?......................................
....

20   Would you like to know and understand more about Europe?
[ ]yes   [ ]no   [ ]not bothered

21   Please give reasons for your answer in question 20

22   From the following list of issues choose 10 which you think are the most important *in Britain*. Please put them in order of importance (i.e. Letter A is the most important issue)

peace	employment	corruption
immigration	asylum	food regulation
pollution	crime	drugs
prosperity	European unity	terrorism
race relations	Bosnia	third world
the family	justice	road safety

A............
B............
C............
D............
E............
F............
G............
H............
I............
J............
Are there any other issues which you feel are important in
Britain?..

23   Do you think that the following issues should be dealt with by the British Government or
by the European Community?

defence	[ ] British government	[ ] EC
employment	[ ] British government	[ ] EC
immigration	[ ] British government	[ ] EC
pollution	[ ] British government	[ ] EC
health education	[ ] British government	[ ] EC
crime	[ ] British government	[ ] EC
drugs	[ ] British government	[ ] EC
equal opportunities	[ ] British government	[ ] EC
race relations	[ ] British government	[ ] EC
Bosnia	[ ] British government	[ ] EC
third world	[ ] British government	[ ] EC
the family	[ ] British government	[ ] EC
justice	[ ] British government	[ ] EC
terrorism	[ ] British government	[ ] EC
anything else you feel strongly about:		
....	[ ] British government	[ ] EC

24   Do you think of yourself as European?
[ ]yes, totally   [ ] only partly   [ ] not at all

25   Do you think of yourself as British?
[ ]yes, totally   [ ] only partly   [ ] not at all

26   The following changes have already happened or may happen as a result of closer European unity. What are your feelings about each one?
    A   the Pound (£) is replaced by the Ecu (a common currency for the whole of the EC)
      [ ]in favour   [ ] against   [ ] not bothered
    B   more decisions affecting your life are taken in Strasbourg rather than in London
      [ ]in favour   [ ] against   [ ] not bothered
    C   citizens of the EC are able to work without restriction in any member country
      [ ]in favour   [ ] against   [ ] not bothered
    D   citizens of the EC are able to vote in elections in the country they live irrespective of their nationality
      [ ]in favour   [ ] against   [ ] not bothered
    E   much greater uniformity of education and training across countries in the community
      [ ]in favour   [ ] against   [ ] not bothered

27   Which EC languages do you think all pupils in the community should learn in school?

True or False? Read these statements about Europe and write T or F in the brackets after each one

1.   There are 12 member states of the EC.   [ ]
2.   Austria is a member state of the EC.   [ ]
3.   The next elections to the European Parliament will be held in June 1994.   [ ]
4.   Greece is a member state of the EC.   [ ]
5.   Luxembourg is the name of a city.   [ ]
6.   Maastricht is a town in Holland where the treaty on European Union
     was signed in 1992.   [ ]
7.   Jacques Delors is President of the European Parliament.   [ ]
8.   Belgium, Denmark, Holland, Spain and the UK have all got monarchies.   [ ]
9.   Dutch is one of 3 official languages spoken in Belgium.   [ ]
10. The ECU is worth less than 50p.   [ ]
11. The Greek currency is called the bouzouki.   [ ]
12. The European Central Bank will be situated in Frankfurt, Germany.   [ ]
13. The country with the largest population in the EC is Germany.   [ ]
14. A Briton who wants to work in France for longer than a year has to
     obtain a work permit.   [ ]
15. The EC has the ultimate say in issues regarding road safety.   [ ]
16. It is an EC regulation that all pupils must learn at least one foreign language
     at school.   [ ]
17. The French equivalent of 'A' levels is called the 'BACCALAUREAT'.   [ ]
18. The EC intends to introduce a common system of school examinations
     for all member states.   [ ]
19. The UK cannot send troops to fight a war zone (e.g. Bosnia) without
     the consent of the European Parliament.   [ ]
20. The fall of the Berlin wall signified the end of the Second World War   [ ]

Appendix A2: CRMLE Student Teacher Questionnaire

PGCE Student Questionnaire

European Awareness

NAME   SEX

MAIN METHOD   AGE

PLEASE NOTE! For the purposes of this study, we are not concerned with Europe as defined by the EC, but with its wider geographical context.

Please indicate, by circling the appropriate number, whether you agree or disagree with the following statements:

    Key
    1 Strongly agree
    2 Agree
    3 No opinion
    4 Disagree
    5 Strongly disagree

1.   I believe that Britain should cooperate with other European countries.
     a) politically   1   2   3   4   5
     b) economically   1   2   3   4   5
     c) culturally   1   2   3   4   5
     d) with regard to social legislation   1   2   3   4   5

2. Britain should bring its own practices into line with other European countries with regard to

a) the electoral system	1	2	3	4	5
b) the legal system	1	2	3	4	5
c) health and NI	1	2	3	4	5
d) educational qualifications	1	2	3	4	5
e) employment law	1	2	3	4	5
f) equal opportunities legislation	1	2	3	4	5

3. European awareness should permeate all subjects in the curriculum.
   1   2   3   4   5

4. The history, geography and cultural background of other European countries should form a significant part of the National Curriculum.
   1   2   3   4   5

5. It should be compulsory for children in schools to learn at least one European language (other than English).
   1   2   3   4   5

6. All British pupils should have the opportunity to visit another European country.
   1   2   3   4   5

7. All British students in HE should have the opportunity to study for part of their course in another European country.
   1   2   3   4   5

8. Have you had the opportunity to consider the European dimension during the course of your PGCE year?
   Yes/No

If yes, please tick the areas where you were able to consider the European dimension.
If no, go to question 9 below.

   a) Subject method work
   b) Educational studies work
      (i.e. lectures, seminars, tutorials, short courses)
   c) Teaching experience / Practice school(s)
      Primary
      Secondary
   d) Assessed work
      (i.e. essays, project work, teaching materials)
   e) Other (i.e. WIS)
      Please specify

9. To what extent do you understand the position of the European dimension within the National Curriculum?
   Fully confident
   Confident
   Uncertain
   Not at all sure

10. Did you include any aspect of the European dimension in your own teaching during teaching practice?
    Yes/No
    If yes, please specify

11.   To what extent do you intend to include any aspects of the European dimension
      in your future teaching?
      As a regular feature
      Occasionally
      Not at all
      If yes, please specify how

12.   Would you ever consider seeking a teaching post in a European country other
      than Britain?
      Yes/No

Finally, please add any comments or suggestions you may have concerning inclusion of a European dimension in future PGCE courses.

Appendix A3: CRMLE Questionnaire for Headteachers and School Governors: The European Dimension in Education

1.   Do you consider a European Dimension in Education to be a worthwhile addition
     to the curriculum? Please comment.

2.   Do you think that the teaching of the ED should be about:
     awareness of opportunities   yes [ ]   no [ ]
     awareness of European Issues   yes [ ]   no [ ]
     European Citizenship   yes [ ]   no [ ]

3.   Do you think that to teach about European Citizenship might lead to political
     indoctrination? Please comment.

4.   Which of the approaches to the ED outlined on the attached sheet would you
     feel were acceptable in your school? Please tick more than one if you feel more
     than one is acceptable:
     1 [ ]   2 [ ]   3 [ ]   4 [ ]   5 [ ]
     Please add comments:

5.   Do you think the pupils in your school should be encouraged to adopt more of
     a dual identity? (e.g. English/British *and* European). Please comment:

6.   Do you agree that, in discussions about social issues, pupils should be encouraged
     to examine solutions at a local level, a national level and a European level?

7.   Would you favour a ED input which stressed the *convergence* of European
     cultures rather than the *divergence* of European cultures?

Please add any other comments regarding the part that education should play in the development of the European Union:

Optional response (please only give this information if you are entirely happy to do so)
Are you
      a teacher governor   [ ]
      a parent governor   [ ]
      a headteacher   [ ]
      a co-opted governor   [ ]
      other   [ ]

APPENDIX B: PUPIL QUESTIONNAIRE DATA TABLES

(In all cases, N represents the total number of responses of a given type for each question.)

B1: Summaries of sample

Table B1.1   *Summary of total sample by country*

Country	N	%
England	554	41.4
France	180	13.5
Spain	171	12.8
Germany	175	13.1
Italy	140	10.5
Netherlands	117	8.8
Total	1337	

Table B1.2   *Summary of total sample by sex*

Sex	N	%
Male	649	48.7
Female	684	51.3

Number of observations missing: 4

Table B1.3   *Summary of total sample by ethnic background*

Ethnic origin	N	%
Afro-Caribbean	21	1.6
Asian	100	7.5
White	1071	80.8
Other	133	10

Number of observations missing: 12

Table B1.4　*Summary of total sample by parental occupation*

	N	%
A	42	3.4
B	326	26.4
C1	408	33
C2	320	25.9
D	91	7.4
Unemployed, retired or housewife	50	4

Number of observations missing: 12

B2: Data relating to pupils' experience of travel

Table B2.1　*Sum total and percentage for each country of pupils' travel experience within Europe* (Question 8)

	Travelled within Europe		Not travelled within Europe	
	N	%	N	%
England	407	73.9	144	26.1
France	156	86.7	24	13.3
Germany	161	92	14	8
Italy	78	55.7	62	44.3
Netherlands	112	95.7	5	4.3
Spain	86	50.6	84	49.4
Total	1000	74.8	333	25

Number of observations missing: 4

Table B2.2　*Number and percentage of pupils who have travelled within Europe with family*

No. of visits	N	%
0	426	35.3
1	658	54.5
2	64	5.3
3	59	4.9

Number of observations missing: 130

Table B2.3　*Number and percentage of pupils who have travelled within Europe with friends*

No. of visits	N	%
0	679	56.3
1	306	27.5
2	95	7.9
3	127	10.5

Number of observations missing: 130

Table B2.4 *Number and percentage of pupils who have travelled within Europe with school*

No. of visits	N	%
0	627	51.9
1	332	27.5
2	80	6.6
3	105	8.7
4	17	1.4
5	22	1.8
6	11	0.9
7	5	0.4
8	1	0.1
9	7	0.6

Number of observations missing: 130

Table B2.5 *Number and percentage of pupils per country who have travelled within Europe with family*

No of visits	England		France		Spain		Germany (incomplete)		Italy		Netherlands		Total
	N	%	N	%	N	%	N	%	N	%	N	%	N
0	216	39	32	17.8	95	55.6	13	28.9	62	44.3	8	6.8	426
1	247	44.6	144	80	67	39.2	32	71.1	61	43.6	107	91.5	658
2	52	9.4	2	1.1	3	1.8	0		6	4.3	1	0.9	64
3	39	7	2	1.1	6	3.5	0		11	7.9	1	0.9	59
Total	554		180		171		45		140		117		1207

Table B2.6 *Number and percentage of pupils per country who have travelled within Europe with friends*

No of visits	England		France		Spain		Germany (incomplete)		Italy		Netherlands		Total
	N	%	N	%	N	%	N	%	N	%	N	%	N
0	306	55.2	89	49.4	135	78.9	37	82.2	93	66.4	19	16.2	679
1	96	17.3	74	41.1	28	16.4	8	17.8	24	17.1	76	65	306
2	44	7.9	8	4.4	6	3.5	0		18	12.9	19	16.2	95
3	108	19.5	9	5	2	1.2	0		5	3.6	3	2.6	127
Total	554		180		171		45		140		117		1207

Table B2.7 *Number and percentage of pupils per country who have travelled within Europe with school*

No of visits	England		France		Germany (incomplete)		Italy		Netherlands		Spain		Total
	N	%	N	%	N	%	N	%	N	%	N	%	N
0	226	40.8	87	48.3	42	93.3	110	78.6	25	21.4	137	80.1	627
1	130	23.5	90	50	3	6.7	20	14.3	60	51.3	29	17	332
2	67	12.1					1	0.7	8	6.8	4	2.3	80
3	68	12.3	3	1.7			9	6.4	24	20.5	1	0.6	105
4	17	3.1											17
5	22	4											22
6	11	2											11
7	5	0.9											5
8	1	0.2											1
9	7	1.3											7
Total	554		180		45		140		117		171		1207

B3: Data relating to information about Europe

Table B3.1 *Breakdown by country of how well informed pupils said they were about Europe* (Question 9)

Responses	England N	%	France N	%	Germany N	%	Italy N	%	Netherlands N	%	Spain N	%
Very well informed	19	3.4	5	2.8	4	2.3	4	2.9	3	2.6	2	1.2
Quite well informed	293	53.1	117	65.4	95	55.6	86	61.4	89	76.7	47	27.5
Not well informed	215	38.9	55	30.7	71	41.5	46	32.9	24	20.7	112	65.5
Not at all informed	25	4.5	2	1.1	1	0.6	4	2.9	0		10	5.8

Number of observations missing: 8

Table B3.2 *Cross-tabulation of responses to the question: 'How well informed do you think you are about Europe?' With quiz scores* (Question 9)

Scores /20	Very well informed N	%	Quite well informed N	%	Not well informed N	%	Not at all informed N	%
0			9	64.3	4	28.6	1	7.1
1			2	100				
2	1	20	1	20	2	40	1	20
3			8	61.5	5	38.5		
4	1	7.7	2	15.4	9	69.2	1	7.7
5			6	37.5	10	62.5		
6			10	52.6	9	47.4		
7	1	2.1	19	40.4	25	53.2	2	4.3
8	4	4.9	27	32.9	45	54.9	6	7.3
9			73	59.3	50	40.7		
10	3	1.9	82	50.6	72	44.4	5	3.1
11	7	3.2	119	53.6	86	38.7	10	4.5
12	4	2.1	103	54.5	78	41.3	4	2.1
13	2	1.2	102	62.6	53	32.5	6	3.7
14	8	5.6	85	59.9	45	31.7	4	2.8
15	3	4.4	45	66.2	19	27.9	1	1.5
16	2	6.1	24	72.7	6	18.2	1	3
17	1	8.3	7	58.3	4	33.3		
18			2	66.7	1	33.3		
19			1	100				

Number of observations missing: 8

Table B3.3 *Number and percentage of pupils per country who believe they have gained their knowledge about Europe from school* (Question 10)

	England N	%	France N	%	Germany N	%	Italy N	%	Netherlands N	%	Spain N	%	Total N
None	45	8.2	4	2.3	5	2.9	6	4.3	2	1.8	30	18.3	92
A little	236	43.2	72	40.7	98	56	55	39.9	46	40.7	103	62.8	610
Most	230	42.1	94	53.1	68	38.9	71	51.4	63	55.8	28	17.1	554
All	35	6.4	7	4	4	2.3	6	4.3	2	1.8	3	1.8	57
Total	546		177		175		138		113		164		1313

Table B3.4   *Number and percentage of pupils per country who believe they have gained their knowledge about Europe from family* (Question 11)

	England		France		Germany		Italy		Netherlands		Spain		Total
	N	%	N	%	N	%	N	%	N	%	N	%	N
None	73	13.7	11	6.3	8	4.6	10	7.3	7	6.1	19	11.9	128
A little	333	62.7	93	53.1	113	64.9	81	59.1	79	69.3	109	68.6	808
Most	117	22	63	36	53	30.5	41	29.9	28	24.6	29	18.2	331
All	8	1.5	8	4.6	0		5	3.6			2	1.3	23
Total	531		175		174		137		114		159		1290

Table B3.5   *Number and percentage of pupils per country who believe they have gained their knowledge about Europe from the media* (Question 12)

	England		France		Germany		Italy		Netherlands		Spain		Total
	N	%	N	%	N	%	N	%	N	%	N	%	N
None	76	14.4	16	9.1	6	3.5	6	4.4	5	4.4	0		109
A little	218	41.3	46	26.3	61	35.3	54	39.4	59	52.2	38	22.5	476
Most	204	38.6	100	57.1	103	59.5	73	53.3	46	40.7	99	58.6	625
All	30	5.7	13	7.4	3	1.7	4	2.9	3	2.7	32	18.9	85
Total	528		175		173		137		113		169		1295

Table B3.6   *Number and percentage of pupils per country who believe they have gained their knowledge about Europe from friends* (Question 13)

	England		France		Germany		Italy		Netherlands		Spain		Total
	N	%	N	%	N	%	N	%	N	%	N	%	N
None	292	56.6	88	52.7	85	49.1	69	51.5	49	45.4	97	61.8	680
A little	200	38.8	69	41.3	84	48.6	61	45.5	58	53.7	58	36.9	530
Most	22	4.3	9	5.4	3	1.7	1	0.7	1	0.9	2	1.3	38
All	2	0.4	1	0.6	1	0.6	3	2.2	0		0		7
Total	516		167		173		134		108		157		1255

Table B3.7   *Number and percentage of pupils per country who believe they have gained their knowledge about Europe from travel* (Question 14)

	England		France		Germany		Italy		Netherlands		Spain		Total
	N	%	N	%	N	%	N	%	N	%	N	%	N
None	150	28.8	48	28.4	31	18.1	58	45	12	10.7	104	66.7	403
A little	231	44.3	87	51.5	88	51.5	48	37.2	63	56.3	44	28.2	561
Most	128	24.6	31	18.3	46	26.9	19	14.7	36	32.1	7	4.5	267
All	12	2.3	3	1.8	6	3.5	4	3.1	1	0.9	1	0.6	27
Total	521		169		171		129		112		156		1258

Table B3.8 *Number and percentage of pupils per country who believe they have gained their knowledge about Europe from relatives or friends living abroad* (Question 15)

	England		France		Germany		Italy		Netherlands		Spain		Total
	N	%	N	%	N	%	N	%	N	%	N	%	N
None	251	48.4	54	32.3	89	51.7	59	45.7	64	57.7	101	63.9	618
A little	195	37.6	75	44.9	56	32.6	50	38.8	39	35.1	48	30.4	463
Most	59	11.4	31	18.6	26	15.1	15	11.6	8	7.2	8	5.1	147
All	14	2.7	7	4.2	1	0.6	5	3.9			1	0.6	28
Total	519		167		172		129		111		158		1256

Table B3.9 *Totals of responses to the question 'How often would you say you gained knowledge or understanding about Europe in school?'* (Question 17)

Frequency	N	%
Daily	58	4.4
A few lessons a week	485	36.6
Once a week	148	11.2
Once every few weeks	196	14.8
A few times a term	101	7.6
Once a term	42	3.2
Never or almost never	131	9.9
I don't know	165	12.4

Number of observations missing: 11

Table B3.10 *Totals of responses to the question 'How much knowledge or understanding about Europe do you gain from [Geography]?'* (Question 18)

Amount	N	%
None	168	13.3
A little	102	8.1
Some	400	31.7
A lot	593	47

Number of observations missing: 74

Table B3.11 *Totals of responses to the question 'How much knowledge or understanding about Europe do you gain from [History]?'* (Question 18)

Amount	N	%
None	194	15.2
A little	207	16.3
Some	491	38.6
A lot	381	29.9

Number of observations missing: 64

Table B3.12 *Totals of responses to the question 'How much knowledge or understanding about Europe do you gain from [Maths]?'* (Question 18)

Amount	N	%
None	1064	82.3
A little	147	11.4
Some	34	2.6
A lot	48	3.7

Number of observations missing: 44

Table B3.13 *Totals of responses to the question 'How much knowledge or understanding about Europe do you gain from [Modern Languages]?'* (Question 18)

Amount	N	%
None	144	11
A little	379	29
Some	452	34.6
A lot	332	25.4

Number of observations missing: 30

Table B3.14 *Totals of responses to the question 'How much knowledge or understanding about Europe do you gain from [Science]?'* (Question 18)

Amount	N	%
None	764	58.9
A little	347	26
Some	145	11.2
A lot	41	3.1

Number of observations missing: 40

Table B3.15 *Totals of responses to the question 'How much knowledge or understanding about Europe do you gain from [Sport]?'* (Question 18)

Amount	N	%
None	1014	80
A little	144	11.4
Some	64	5
A lot	45	3.5

Number of observations missing: 70

Table B3.16 *Totals of responses to the question 'How much knowledge or understanding about Europe do you gain from [Own language lessons]?'* (Question 18)

Amount	N	%
None	464	36.7
A little	487	38.5
Some	234	18.5
A lot	79	6.2

Number of observations missing: 73

B4: Data relating to language learning

Table B4.1   *Main modern foreign languages mentioned in response to the question 'What languages have you been taught at school?' (Question 19)*

Foreign language taught	No. of pupils mentioning the language	% of total sample
English	829	62
French	797	59.6
German	695	52
Italian	17	1.3
Russian	16	1.2
Spanish	78	5.8

Table B4.2   *Main modern foreign languages mentioned in response to the question 'Which EC languages do you think all pupils in the community should learn in school?' (Question 27)*

Languages which should be taught	No. of pupils mentioning the language	% of total sample
English	834	62.4
Dutch	17	1.3
French	737	55.1
German	548	41
Italian	109	8.2
Russian	13	1
Spanish	346	25.8

B5: Data relating to pupils' expressions of interest in learning more about Europe

Table B5.1   *Totals and percentages of responses to the question 'Would you like to know and understand more about Europe?' (Question 20)*

Response	N	%
Yes	896	67.4
No	70	5.3
Not bothered	364	27.4

Number of observations missing: 7

Table B5.2   *Breakdown of total responses to Question 20 by whether or not pupils had travelled within Europe*

Response	Travelled within Europe		Not travelled within Europe	
	N	%	N	%
Yes	658	65.8	235	72.1
No	49	4.9	20	6.1
Not bothered	293	29.3	71	21.8

Table B5.3 *Breakdown of total responses to Question 20 by quiz scores*

Score /20	Yes N	%	No N	%	Not bothered N	%
0	8	57.1	3	21.4	3	21.4
1			1	50	1	50
2	2	40			3	60
3	9	64.3			5	35.7
4	9	69.2			4	30.8
5	11	68.8			5	31.3
6	10	52.6	2	10.5	7	36.8
7	29	61.7	3	6.4	15	31.9
8	53	65.4	4	4.9	24	29.6
9	80	65.6	5	4.1	37	30.3
10	117	72.2	8	4.9	37	22.8
11	153	68.6	13	5.8	57	25.6
12	121	64.7	12	6.4	54	28.9
13	112	67.5	8	4.8	46	27.7
14	94	65.7	5	3.5	44	30.8
15	55	82.1	3	4.5	9	13.4
16	26	78.8			7	21.2
17	8	66.7	3	25	1	8.3
18	1	33.3			2	66.7
19					1	100

Number of observations missing: 8

Table B5.4 *Breakdown of total responses to Question 20 by sex*

Response	Males N	%	Females N	%
Yes	398	61.5	495	72.9
No	56	8.7	170	25
Not bothered	193	29.8	14	2.1

Table B5.5 *Breakdown of total responses to Question 20 by ethnic origin*

Response	Afro-Caribbean N	%	Asian N	%	White N	%	Other N	%
Yes	10	47.6	65	65.7	706	66.2	106	80.9
No	2	9.5	7	7.1	57	5.4	3	2.3
Not bothered	9	42.9	27	27.3	304	28.5	22	16.8

B6: Data relating to pupils' views on collaboration within the EU

Table B6.1   *Percentages of total responses to the question: 'Do you think that the following issues should be dealt with by the national government or by the European Community?' (Question 23)*

Issue	EC level	National level	Both
Bosnia	85.4	10.9	3.7
The Third World	84.6	10.3	5.1
Race relations	68.7	26.6	4.8
Immigration	67.3	30.7	1.5
Drugs	61.2	33.9	3.9
Equal opportunities	58.3	36.4	3.8
Pollution	56	40	4
Terrorism	54.2	39.5	4.8
Defence	46.4	47.3	1.9
Crime	38.9	57	4.1
Health education	35.1	62.1	2.8
Justice	32.5	63.4	4.1
Employment	25.5	72.3	2.2
The family	16.6	80.1	3.1

Table B6.2   *Total summary and breakdown by country of attitudes to changes in EU policy (Question 26)*

Change	In favour (%)	Not bothered (%)	Against (%)
The national currency is replaced by the ECU	England 20.7 France 52.2 Germany 29.7 Italy 83.6 Netherlands 49.6 Spain 45.3	England 33.4 France 29.2 Germany 22.7 Italy 3.6 Netherlands 17.1 Spain 38.2	England 45.9 France 18.5 Germany 47.7 Italy 12.9 Netherlands 33.3 Spain 16.5
	Total 38.5	Total 27.5	Total 34
More decisions affecting your life are taken in Strasbourg	England 7.5 France 30.3 Germany 14.6 Italy 30.2 Netherlands 12 Spain 7.8	England 31.8 France 58.4 Germany 62 Italy 20.1 Netherlands 22.2 Spain 43.4	England 60.7 France 11.2 Germany 23.4 Italy 49.6 Netherlands 65.8 Spain 48.2
	Total 14.3	Total 38.7	Total 46.9
Working without restriction in EU member states	England 42 France 67.4 Germany 67.8 Italy 88.6 Netherlands 60.7 Spain 71.3	England 35.6 France 24.2 Germany 12.9 Italy 0.7 Netherlands 15.4 Spain 20.5	England 22.2 France 8.4 Germany 19.3 Italy 10.7 Netherlands 23.9 Spain 7.6
	Total 59.1	Total 23.7	Total 17
EU citizens able to vote in country of residence regardless of nationality	England 48.9 France 52.2 Germany 63.7 Italy 70 Netherlands 57.3 Spain 47.9	England 32.9 France 20.8 Germany 13.5 Italy 6.4 Netherlands 14.5 Spain 29	England 18.2 France 27 Germany 22.8 Italy 23.6 Netherlands 28.2 Spain 23.1
	Total 54	Total 23.8	Total 22

Greater uniformity of education and training	England 48.4	England 43.6	England 8
	France 55.9	France 40.1	France 4
	Germany 57.1	Germany 31.8	Germany 11.2
	Italy 94.2	Italy 4.3	Italy 1.4
	Netherlands 59	Netherlands 16.2	Netherlands 24.8
	Spain 82.9	Spain 15.9	Spain 1.2
	Total 60.7	Total 31.5	Total 7.8

Table B6.3 *Breakdown by sex of attitudes to EU policy changes* (Question 26)

| | In favour | | | | Not bothered | | | | Against | | | |
| | Males | | Females | | Males | | Females | | Males | | Females | |
Policy change	N	%	N	%	N	%	N	%	N	%	N	%
The national currency is replaced by the ECU	220	34.2	230	34.1	168	26.1	193	28.6	255	39.7	252	37.3
More decisions affecting your life are taken in Strasbourg	316	49.5	300	44.4	228	35.7	282	41.8	95	14.9	93	13.8
Working without restriction in EU member states	128	19.9	97	14.3	143	22.2	172	25.3	373	58	409	60.2
EU citizens able to vote in country of residence regardless of nationality	178	27.8	113	16.6	159	24.8	157	23.1	204	47.4	410	60.2
Greater uniformity of education and training	65	10.2	38	5.6	207	32.3	210	30.9	368	57.5	431	63.5

B7: Data relating to pupils' views on identity

Table B7.1 *Question 24: 'Do you think of yourself as European?'*

| Thought of themselves as European | England | | France | | Germany | | Italy | | Spain | | Netherlands | | Total | |
	N	%	N	%	N	%	N	%	N	%	N	%	N	%
Not at all	218	39.8	31	17.4	18	10.5	6	4.3	11	6.4	3	2.6	287	21.7
Only partly	228	41.6	73	41	45	26.3	57	41	43	25.1	8	7	454	34.3
Yes, totally	102	18.6	74	41.6	107	62.6	76	54.7	117	68.4	105	90.4	581	43.9

Number of observations missing: 14

Table B7.2 *Question 24: 'Do you think of yourself as European?'* (Ethnic)

| Thought of themselves as European | Afro-Caribbean | | Asian | | White | | Other | |
	N	%	N	%	N	%	N	%
Not at all	11	55	46	46.5	214	20.2	13	9.8
Only partly	8	40	43	43.4	337	31.8	61	46.2
Yes, totally	1	5	10	10.1	509	47.9	58	43.9

Number of observations missing: 26

Table B7.3　*Breakdown of Question 24 (European identity) by Question 8 (travel)–Total responses*

Thought of themselves as European	Travelled within Europe		Not travelled within Europe	
	N	%	N	%
Not at all	198	20	88	26.4
Only partly	350	35.4	103	31.3
Yes, totally	441	44.6	139	42.2
Column total	989	73.9	330	24.7

Number of observations missing: 111

Table B7.4　*Breakdown of Question 24 (European identity) by parental occupation–Total responses*

Thought of themselves as European	A		B		C1		C2		D		Unemployed, retired, housewife		Row total	
	N	%	N	%	N	%	N	%	N	%	N	%	N	%
Not at all	12	28.6	53	16.5	75	18.5	70	22.2	23	25.3	22	44.9	255	20.8
Only partly	10	23.8	101	31.4	146	36	113	35.8	36	39.6	11	22.4	417	34
Yes, totally	20	47.6	168	52.2	185	43.5	133	42.1	32	35.2	16	32.7	554	45.2

Table B7.5　*Total responses to the question 'Do you think of yourself as British, French, etc. ?' (Question 25)*

Thought of themselves as British etc.	N	%
Not at all	71	5.4
Only partly	261	19.7
Yes, totally	993	74.9

Number of observations missing: 12

Table B7.6　*Breakdown of Question 25 (national identity) by country*

Thought of themselves as British etc.	England		France		Germany		Italy		Netherlands		Spain	
	N	%	N	%	N	%	N	%	N	%	N	%
Not at all	22	4	12	6.7	32	18.7	2	1.4	0		3	1.8
Only partly	141	25.7	29	16.2	56	32.7	19	13.7	7	6	9	5.3
Yes, totally	386	70.3	138	77.1	83	48.5	118	84.9	109	94	159	93

Number of observations missing: 12

Table B7.7　*Breakdown of Question 25 (national identity) by ethnic origin*

	Afro-Caribbean		Asian		White		Other	
	N	%	N	%	N	%	N	%
Not at all	2	10	23	23	33	3.1	11	8.3
Only partly	10	50	50	50	163	15.4	37	28
Yes, totally	8	40	27	27	865	81.5	84	63.6

Number of observations missing: 24

Table B7.8 *Breakdown of Question 25 (national identity) by travel*

Thought of themselves as British etc.	Travelled within Europe		Not travelled within Europe	
	N	%	N	%
Not at all	55	5.6	16	4.8
Only partly	199	20.1	61	18.4
Yes, totally	736	74.4	254	76.7
Column total	990	74.9	331	25

Number of observations missing: 16

Table B7.9 *Breakdown of Question 25 (national identity) by parental occupation*

Thought of themselves as British etc.	A		B		C1		C2		D		Unemployed, retired, housewife	
	N	%	N	%	N	%	N	%	N	%	N	%
Not at all	2	4.8	18	5.6	15	3.7	14	4.4	11	12.1	3	6
Only partly	4	9.5	53	16.4	81	20	63	19.8	26	28.6	12	24
Yes, totally	36	85.7	252	78	309	76.3	241	75.8	54	59.3	35	70

Number of observations missing: 108

Table B7.10 *Breakdown of Question 25 (national identity) by sex*

Thought of themselves as British etc.	Males		Females	
	N	%	N	%
Not at all	37	5.8	34	5
Only partly	126	19.6	134	19.8
Yes, totally	480	74.7	510	75.2

Number of observations missing: 16

Table B7.11 *Breakdown by sex of responses expressing total or no European or national identity*

	Males (%)	Females (%)
Felt totally 'national'	74.7	75.2
Felt totally European	40.5	47.3
Felt not at all 'national'	5.8	5
Felt not at all European	25.7	17.8

Table B7.12 *Breakdown of responses to the question 'Do you think of yourself as European?' by ethnic background of English sample only*

Thought of themselves as European	Afro-Caribbean		Asian		White		Other	
	N	%	N	%	N	%	N	%
Not at all	8	57.1	36	46.8	170	38.5	4	25
Only partly	6	42.9	35	45.5	176	39.9	11	68.8
Yes, totally	0		6	7.8	95	21.5	16	6.3

Number of observations missing: 6

Table B7.13   *Breakdown of responses to the question 'Do you think of yourself as British?' by ethnic background of English sample only*

Thought of themselves as British	Afro-Caribbean		Asian		White		Other	
	N	%	N	%	N	%	N	%
Not at all	2	14.3	8	10.3	10	2.3	2	12.5
Only partly	7	50	45	57.7	82	18.6	7	43.8
Yes, totally	5	35.7	25	32.1	349	79.1	7	43.8

Number of observations missing: 5

APPENDIX C: STUDENT TEACHER QUESTIONNAIRE DATA TABLES

Table C1   *Breakdown of student ages in percentages*

Age band	% of student sample
20–23	52
24–29	30
30+	18

Table C2   *Breakdown of student method subjects on PGCE course in percentages*

Subject	% of student sample
Science	20.2
Mathematics	19.4
Modern Languages	19.3
English	18.6
Geography	10.1
History	9.3
Classics	3.1
Total	100.0

Table C3   *Comparison of different age groups' responses to statement: 'Britain should bring its own practices into line with other European countries with regard to equal opportunities legislation'*

Age group	Agree (%)	Disagree (%)	No opinion (%)
20–23	82.3	5.9	11.8
24–29	60.5	29	10.5
30+	73.9	4.4	21.7

Table C4   *Degrees of agreement between linguists and non-linguists on pupils visiting other European countries*

	Strongly agree (%)	Agree (%)
Linguists	88	12
Non-linguists	51.4	44.8

Table C5 *Percentages of students from different subject areas incorporating a European dimension in their school-based work*

Subject	Autumn term teaching experience %	Spring term teaching practice %
English	25	20.8
Mathematics	12	25
Science	26.9	23.1
Geography	76.9	83.3
History	58.3	66.7
Classics	75	100
Modern Languages	84	91.7

APPENDIX D: SCHOOL GOVERNING BODY QUESTIONNAIRE DATA TABLES

Table D1 *The European dimension should be about ...*
(N=44)

	Yes	No	No response
Awareness of opportunities	42	1	1
Awareness of European issues	43	1	
European citizenship	37	4	3

Table D3 *Number of respondents who thought approaches in Table D2 acceptable*

Approach 1	30
Approach 2	19
Approach 3	36
Approach 4	36
Approach 5	35
Total	156

APPENDIX E: MAASTRICHT TREATY ARTICLES RELATING TO EDUCATION AND CITIZENSHIP

E.1: Education, vocational training and youth

Article 126

1   The Community shall contribute to the development of quality education by encouraging cooperation between Member States and, if necessary, by supporting and supplementing their action, while fully respecting the responsibility of the Member States for the content of teaching and the organization of education systems and their cultural and linguistic diversity.

Table D2   *Approaches to the European dimension in education*

1	2	3	4	5
Actively promoting citizenship	Examining the institutions for their effectiveness	Historical perspective of the EU 1950–92	School trips for language learning	Historical and geographical knowledge of Europe
Active involvement in principles of democracy and social justice	Making judgements about speed of unification	Understanding the workings of the EU institutions	Language learning for jobs, business and tourism purposes	
Understanding of rights and obligations	Discussing pros and cons of federalism	Keeping abreast of European Union developments		
Debating political issues within a *European Union* context	A European dimension in history, geography, MFL and English	School trips to other European countries for cultural awareness and cultural comparisons		
Involvement in intra-European school projects	Extended language learning, e.g. geography taught in French	Language learning in a cultural context		
Examining the media for bias		A European dimension in history, geography and languages		
Analysing various levels of decision-making to see where decisions are best made				
A European dimension in every school subject and/or specific course in PSE programme				

2   Community action shall be aimed at:
   -   developing the European dimension in education, particularly through the teaching and dissemination of the languages of the Member States;
   -   encouraging mobility of students and teachers, inter alia by encouraging the academic recognition of diplomas and periods of study;
   -   promoting cooperation between educational establishments;
   -   developing exchanges of information and experience on issues common to the education systems of the Member States;
   -   encouraging the development of youth exchanges and of exchanges of socio-educational instructors;
   -   encouraging the development of distance education.
3   In order to contribute to the achievement of the objectives referred to in this Article, the Council:
   -   acting in accordance with the procedure referred to in Article 189b, after consulting the Economic and Social Committee and the Committee of the Regions, shall adopt incentive measures, excluding any harmonization of the laws and regulations of the Member States;
   -   acting by a qualified majority on a proposal from the Commission, shall adopt recommendations.

Article 127

1   The Community shall implement a vocational training policy which shall support and supplement the action of the Member States, while fully respecting the responsibility of the Member States for the content and organization of vocational training.
2   Community action shall aim to:
   -   facilitate adaptation to industrial changes, in particular through vocational training and retraining;
   -   improve initial and continuing vocational training in order to facilitate vocational integration and reintegration into the labour market;
   -   facilitate access to vocational training and encourage mobility of instructors and trainees and particularly young people;
   -   stimulate cooperation on training between educational or training establishments and firms;
   -   develop exchanges of information and experience on issues common to the training systems of the Member States.
3   The Community and the Member States shall foster cooperation with third countries and the competent international organizations in the sphere of vocational training.
4   The Council, acting in accordance with the procedure referred to in Article 189c and after consulting the Economic and Social Committee, shall adopt measures to contribute to the achievement of the objectives referred to in this Article, excluding any harmonization of the laws and regulations of the Member States.

E2: Citizenship of the Union

Article 8

1   Citizenship of the Union is hereby established. Every person holding the nationality of a Member State shall be a citizen of the Union.
2   Citizens of the Union shall enjoy the rights conferred by this Treaty and shall be subject to the duties imposed thereby.

Article 8a

1   Every citizen of the Union shall have the right to move and reside freely within the territory of the Member States, subject to the limitations and conditions laid down in this Treaty and by the measures adopted to give it effect.
2   The Council may adopt provisions with a view to facilitating the exercise of the rights referred to in paragraph 1; save as otherwise provided in this Treaty, the Council shall act unanimously on a proposal from the Commission and after obtaining the assent of the European Parliament.

Article 8b

1   Every citizen of the Union residing in a Member State of which he is not a national shall have the right to vote and to stand as a candidate at municipal elections in the Member State in which he resides, under the same conditions as nationals of that State. This right shall be exercised subject to detailed arrangements to be adopted before 31 December 1994 by the Council, acting unanimously on a proposal from the Commission and after consulting the European Parliament; these arrangements may provide for derogations where warranted by problems specific to a Member State.
2   Without prejudice to Article 138(3) and to the provisions adopted for its implementation, every citizen of the Union residing in a Member State of which he is not a national shall have the right to vote and to stand as a candidate in elections to the European Parliament in the Member State in which he resides, under the same conditions as nationals of that State. This right shall be exercised subject to detailed arrangements to be adopted before 31 December 1993 by the Council, acting unanimously on a proposal from the Commission and after consulting the European Parliament; these arrangements may provide for derogations where warranted by problems specific to a Member State.

Article 8c

Every citizen of the Union shall, in the territory of a third country in which the Member State of which he is a national is not represented, be entitled to protection by the diplomatic or consular authorities of any Member State, on the same conditions as the nationals of that State. Before 31 December 1993, Member States shall establish the necessary rules among themselves and start the international negotiations required to secure this protection.

Article 8d

Every citizen of the Union shall have the right to petition the European Parliament in accordance with Article 138d.

Every citizen of the Union may apply to the Ombudsman established in accordance with Article 138e.

Bibliography

Académie de Rouen (1994) *Plan Académique de Formation 94/95*. Rouen: Académie de Rouen.

Académie de Strasbourg (1994) *Plan Académique de Formation 94/95*. Strasbourg: Académie de Strasbourg.

Adelman, C. and Macaro, E. (1995) 'Curriculum theory and citizenship education: A comparison between England and Italy.' *Curriculum*, **16** (1), 36–46.

Baron, R. and Byrne, D. (1981) *Social Psychology: Understanding Human Interaction*. Boston, Mass.: Allen and Bacon .

Barret, M. and Short, J. (1992) 'Images of European people in a group of 5–10–year–old English schoolchildren.' *British Journal of Developmental Psychology*, **10**, 339–63.

Bayerisches Staatsministerium für Unterricht und Kultur, letter to all schools re 'Gemeinschaft erleben – unser Staat' and 'Europa entdecken – Einheit und Vielfalt.' Munich, 1 June 1992.

Bayerisches Staatsministerium für Unterricht und Kultur, report to the *Sekretariat der ständigen Konferenz der Kultusminister der Länder in der Bundesrepublik*. Munich, 20 August 1990.

Bell, G. H. (1995) *Educating European Citizens*. London: David Fulton.

Bordas, I. and Giles Jones, M. (1993) 'Students' attitudes to Europe: An investigative study.' In M. Montané and I. Bordas (eds) *The European Dimension in Secondary Education*. Barcelona: Collegi de Doctors i Llicenciats en Filosofia i Lletres i en Ciències de Catalunya.

British Broadcasting Corporation (1994) *Teaching Modern Foreign Languages Today*, Programme 1 of 'Teaching Today'. London: BBC Education.

Brock, C and Tulasiewicz, W. (eds) (1994) *Education in a Single Europe*. London: Routledge.

Broeder, P. (1996) *Research Group on Language and Minorities*. Tilburg University (paper given at the University of Reading).

Bruner, J. (1974) *The Relevance of Education*. Harmondsworth: Penguin.

Brynner, J. and Ashford S. (1994) 'Politics and Participation: Some antecedents of young people's attitudes to the political system and political activity.' *European Journal of Social Psychology*, **24**, 223–36.

Buiten, B. (1992) *Het Europees Platform voor het Nederlands onderwijs: Rapport van een evaluatie-onderzoek* [The European Platform for Dutch education: report of an evaluation study]. The Hague: de Roo en Partners.

Byram, M., Esarte-Sarries, V. and Taylor, S. (1991) *Cultural Studies and Language Learning: a research report*. Clevedon: Multilingual Matters.

Byram, M. (1992) 'Foreign language learning for European citizenship.' *Language Learning Journal*, September (6), 10–12.

Carr, W. (1991) 'Education for citizenship.' *British Journal of Educational Studies*, **39**(4), 373–85.

Carter, R., (ed.) (1990) *Knowledge About Language*. Sevenoaks: Hodder & Stoughton.

Central Bureau for Educational Visits and Exchanges (1995) *Teaching Assistants from European Union Member States and from Countries in the European Economic Area*. London.

Central Bureau for Educational Visits and Exchanges (1996) *Eurodesk Information*. London.

Chambers, G. (1994) 'A snapshot in motivation at 10+, 13+ and 16+.' *Language Learning Journal*, March (9), 14–18.

Cunningham, L. (1994) 'Student skills for the New Europe.' HEC Conference Report.

Dahrendorf, R. (1994) 'The changing quality of citizenship.' In B. Van Steenbergen (ed.) *The Condition of Citizenship*. London: Sage.

Davies, I. (1995) *Education for European Citizenship: Values and the Teaching and Learning of History*. York: Department of Educational Studies, University of York.

Dekker, H. (1993) 'European citizenship: A political-psychological analysis.' In M. Montané and I. Bordas (eds) *The European Dimension in Secondary Education*. Barcelona: Collegi de Doctors i Llicenciats en Filosofia i Lletres i en Ciències de Catalunya.

Dekker, H. (1994) 'Socialisation and education of young people for democratic citizenship, theory and research.' In L. Edwards, P. Munn and K. Fogelman (eds) *Education for Democratic Citizenship in Europe*. Lisse: Swets and Zeitlinger, pp. 48–90.

Department of Education (1990) *Modern Foreign Languages for Ages 11 to 16*. London: HMSO.

Department of Education (1991a) *The European Dimension in Education*. London: HMSO.

Department of Education (1991b) *Modern Foreign Languages in the National Curriculum*. London: HMSO.

Department of Education (DFE) (1991c) *History in the National Curriculum*. London: HMSO.

Department of Education (1991d) *Geography in the National Curriculum*. London: HMSO.

Department of Education (1992) *Policy Models: A Guide to Developing and Implementing European Dimension Policies in LEAs, Schools and Colleges*. London: HMSO.

Edgar, N. and Roe, A. (1994) *Europe ... What Everyone Needs to Know*. Cambridge: Pearson.

Edwards, L., Munn, P. and Fogelman, K. (eds) (1994) *Education for Democratic Citizenship in Europe*. Lisse: Swets and Zeitlinger.

EMIE/NFER (Hopkins, K.) (1991) *European Awareness: The LEAs and 1992*. Slough.

Endt, E. and Lenaerts, R. (eds) (1993) 'The European dimension in education.' *Report on the 4th International Symposium*. Netherlands: National Institute for Curriculum Development (SLO).

Engle, S. and Ochoa, A. (1988) *Education for Democratic Citizenship*. New York: Teachers College Press.

European, The (1992) *Maastricht Made Simple. Special Guide No. 1*.

European Commission (1982) *The Young Europeans*. Brussels: European Commission.

European Commission (1989) *Young Europeans in 1987*. Brussels: European Commission.

European Commission (1991a) *Young Europeans in 1990*. Brussels: European Commission.

European Commission (1991b) *First Progress Report on Action Undertaken by the Member States and by the European Community with a View to Strengthening the European Dimension in Education*. Brussels '23 September' SEC (91), ref. no. 1753.

European Commission Task Force for Human Resources, Education, Training and Youth (1993) *Proposal for a Decision of the European Parliament and of the Council Establishing the Community Action Programme 'SOCRATES' (Aims)*. Brussels: European Commission.

European Commission (1994) *Eurobarometer, 41*. Brussels: European Commission.

European Commission (1995a) *1996 European Year of Lifelong Learning: Guide to applicants*. Brussels: European Commission.

European Commission (1995b) *Key Data on Education in the European Union*. Luxembourg: European Commission.

Fanon, F. (1952) *Peau Noire, Masques Blancs*. Paris: du Seuil.

Feneyrou, R. (1993) 'The European dimension in education: questions on its meaning.' In M. Montané and I. Bordas (eds) *The European Dimension in Secondary Education*. Barcelona: Collegi de Doctors i Llicenciats en Filosofia i Lletres i en Ciències de Catalunya, pp. 89–111.

Fletcher, P. and Yamada-Yamamoto, A. (1994) *The Acquisition of English by Japanese-speaking Children Living in Britain*. Final report to the Toyota Foundation. Reading University: Department of Linguistics.

Furnham, A. and Gunter, B. (1989) *The Anatomy of Adolescence: Young People's Social Attitudes in Britain*. London: Routledge.

Gale, P. and Hunt, J. (1993) *Into Europe – Planning and Delivering the Curriculum in the 90s*. Lancaster: Framework .

Goodson, I. F. and McGivney, V. (1985) *European Dimensions and the Secondary School Curriculum*. London: Falmer.

Graham, D. and Tytler, D. (1993) *A Lesson For Us All. The Making of the National Curriculum*. London: Routledge.

Green, S. (1995) 'The European dimension in German schools.' In H. J. Hahn, (ed.) *Germany in the 1990s*. Amsterdam: Rodopi B. V., pp. 147–55.

Gurney, M. (1991) *Personal and Social Education, An Integrated Programme*. Cheltenham: Stanley Thornes.

Habermas, J. (1994) 'Citizenship and national identity.' In B. Van Steenbergen (ed.) *The Condition of Citizenship*. London: Sage.

Hagen, S. (1992) 'Language policy and strategy issues in the new Europe.' *Language Learning Journal*, March, (5), 31–4.

Halman, L. and Ester, P. (1994) 'The ethos of individualism in cross-cultural perspective: exploring the European values data.' Paper presented at the conference: The European Legacy: towards new paradigms, Graz, Austria: International Society for the Study of European Ideas.

Heater, D. and Crick, B. (1977) *Essays on Political Education*. Ringmer: Falmer.

Heater, D. (1990) *Citizenship. The civic ideal in world history, politics and education*. London: Longman.

Heater, D. (1992) 'Education for European citizenship.' *Westminster Studies in Education*. **15**, 53–67.

Hewstone, M. (1986) *Understanding Attitudes to the European Community: A Social-Psychological Study in Four Member States*. Cambridge: Cambridge University Press.

Hopkins, K. *et al.* (1994) *Into the Heart of Europe: The education dimension*. Slough: NFER.

Humberside County Council (1994) *European Awareness County Council Policy Statement and Development Plan*.

Inglehart, R. (1977) *The Silent Revolution: Changing Values and Political Styles among Western Publics*. Princeton, NJ: Princeton University Press.

Inglehart, R. and Reif, K. (1991) 'Analysing trends in West European opinion: The role of the Eurobarometer surveys.' In R. Inglehart and K. Reif (eds) *Eurobarometer: The Dynamics of European Public Opinion. Essays in Honour of Jacques-René Rabier*. London: Macmillan, pp. 1–26.

King, A. S. and Reiss, M. J. (eds) (1993) *The Multicultural Dimension of the National Curriculum*. London: Falmer.

Kirby, M. (1994a) *The European Election*. Cambridge: Pearson.

Kirby, M. (1994b) *The Europe Kit*. Cambridge: Pearson.

Kultusministerkonferenz (1990) *Europa im Unterricht*. Bonn.

Legendre, J. (1995) 'Vers un nouveau contrat pour l'enseignement des langues vivantes.' *Les Rapports du Sénat*, **73**. Paris: Sénat.

Lemarchand, F. and Julié, K. (1991) *Apple Pie*. Paris: Hachette.

Lenning, T. (1995) *The European Graduate Survey*. Stockholm: Universum AB.

Lodge, J. (1993) (ed.) *The European Community and the Challenge of the Future*. London: Pinter.

LOGSE (1990) *see* Ministerio de Educación y Ciencia.

Macaro, E. (1997) *Target Language, Collaborative Learning and Autonomy*. Clevedon: Multilingual Matters (in press).

Macdonald, S. (1993) *Inside Western Europe: Ethnography in Western Europe*. Oxford: Berg.

Maxwell, E. (1994) 'Lighter loads for the class atlas.' *Times Educational Supplement*. 13 May.

McGhie, M. (1993) 'The European Dimension.' In E. Endt and R. Lenaerts (eds) 'The European Dimension in Education.' *Report on the 4th International Symposium*. Netherlands: National Institute for Curriculum Development (SLO).

McLaughlin, T. H. (1992) 'Citizenship, diversity and education: A philosophical perspective.' *Journal of Moral Education*, **21**(3), 235–50.

McLean, M. (1990) *Britain and a Single Market Europe*. London: Kogan Page.

Metropolitan Borough of Knowsley (1994) *European Policy for Schools*. Knowsley.

Ministère de L'Education Nationale (1985) *Collèges: Programmes et Instructions 1985*. Paris: Centre National de Documentation Pédagogique et Ministère de l'Education Nationale.

Ministerio de Educación y Ciencia (1990) *Ley Orgánica de Ordenación General del Sistema Educativo (LOGSE)*. Madrid: Centro de Publicaciones.

Montané, M. and Bordas, I. (eds) (1993) *The European Dimension in Secondary Education*. Barcelona: Collegi de Doctors i Llicenciats en Filosofia i Lletres i en Ciències de Catalunya.

Morrell, F. (1996) *Continent Isolated: A Study of the European Dimension in the National Curriculum in England*. London: Federal Trust for Education and Research.

Moscovici, S. (1981) 'On social representations.' In J. P. Forgas (ed.) *Social Cognition: Perspectives on everyday understanding*. London: Academic Press, pp. 181–209.

Mossuz-Lavau, J. (1991) 'Women and men of Europe today: attitudes towards Europe and politics.' *Women of Europe* (35), 12–21.

Moxon-Browne, E. (1993) 'Social Europe.' In J. Lodge (ed.) *The European Community and the Challenge of the Future*. London: Pinter.

Mulcahy, D. G. (1991) 'In search of the European dimension in education.' *European Journal of Teacher Education*, **14**(3), 213–26.

Mulcahy, D. G. (1992) 'Promoting the European dimension in Irish education.' *Irish Educational Studies*, **11**, 179–90.

National Council for Educational Technology (1995) *Managing I.T.: A Planning Tool for Senior Managers*. Coventry: NCET.

National Curriculum Council (NCC) (1990) *The Whole Curriculum: Curriculum Guidance 3*. York: NCC.

National Curriculum Council (NCC) (1990) *Curriculum Guidance 8: Education for Citizenship*. York: NCC.

National Curriculum Council (1992) *Starting Out with the National Curriculum*. York: NCC.

Neave, G. (1984) *The EEC and Education*. Trentham: Trentham Books.

Newbold, D. (1996) 'European stresses stir controversy.' *Times Educational Supplement*, 19 January.

Office for Official Publications of the European Communities (1992) *Treaty on European Union*. Luxembourg.

Office for Standards in Education (OFSTED) (1993) *Handbook for the Inspection of Schools*. London: HMSO.

Office for Standards in Education (OFSTED) (1995) *Guidance on the Inspection of Secondary Schools*. London: HMSO.

O'Malley, B. (1996) 'Drive on languages runs out of steam.' *Times Educational Supplement*, 2 February.

Orwell, G. (1957) *Selected Essays*. Harmondsworth: Penguin.

Patterson, P. and Sahni, A. (1994) *Choices for Britain: Avon Pilot Evaluation*. Bristol: Public Voice International.

Rayou, P. (1994) 'Of citizens and men: Civic education and political socialisation of pupils at upper secondary schools.' In L. Edwards, P. Munn and K. Fogelman (eds) *Education for Democratic Citizenship in Europe*. Lisse: Swets and Zeitlinger.

Schön, D.A. (1987) *Educating the Reflective Practitioner*. San Francisco: Jossey-Bass.

School Curriculum and Assessment Authority (SCAA) (1994) *The National Curriculum and its Assessment*. London: HMSO.

School Curriculum and Assessment Authority (SCAA) (1995a) *Geography in the National Curriculum*. London: HMSO.

School Curriculum and Assessment Authority (SCAA) (1995b) *History in the National Curriculum*. London: HMSO.

School Curriculum and Assessment Authority (SCAA) (1995c) *Modern Foreign Languages in the National Curriculum*. London: HMSO.

Scottish Consultative Council on the Curriculum (1993) *Thinking European: ideas for integrating a European dimension into the curriculum*. Dundee.

The Scottish Office Education Department (1994) *Scottish Education and the European Community: Policy, Strategy and Practice*. Edinburgh.

Shennan, M. (1991) *Teaching about Europe*. London: Cassell.

Starkey, H. (1995) 'From rhetoric to reality: Starting to implement education for European values.' In G. H. Bell *Educating European Citizens*, London: David Fulton.

Sultana, R. G. (1995) 'A Uniting Europe, a Dividing Education? Supranationalism, Euro-Centrism and the Curriculum.' *International Studies in Sociology of Education*, **5**(2), 115–44.

Tacade (1994) *Skills for Life*. Salford: Tacade.

Taylor, W. H. (1993) 'Educating British children for European citizenship.' *European Journal of Education*, **28**(4), 437–44.

Times Educational Supplement and Centre for Information on Language Teaching (1996) *Survey of Modern Languages in Secondary Schools*. London: CILT.

Tulasiewicz, W. (1993) 'The European dimension and the National Curriculum.' In A. S. King and M. J. Reiss (eds) *The Multicultural Dimension of the National Curriculum*. London: Falmer.

Vaniscotte, F. (1989) *70 Millions d'élèves: L'Europe de l'éducation*. Hatier: Paris.

Waller, R. (1995) 'Taxing polls.' *New Statesman and Society*, 26 May, 8–9.

Whitty, G. and Rowe, G. (1993) 'Five Themes Remain in the Shadows.' *Times Educational Supplement*, 9 April.

Whitty, G., Rowe, G., and Aggleton, P. (1994) 'Subjects and themes in the secondary school curriculum.' In T. Wragg (ed.) *Research Papers in Education, Policy and Practice*, **9**(2), London: Routledge.

Wubbels, T. (1992) 'Taking account of student teachers' preconceptions.' *Teaching and Teacher Education*, **8**(2).

Index